HANDBOOK OF NEUROLINGUISTIC PROGRAMMING

HOW TO PROGRAM YOUR MIND FOR HAPPINESS & SUCCESS

ELLIOTT MIDDLETON PHD

The limits of my language mean the limits of my world.

— LUDWIG WITTGENSTEIN

We are what we repeatedly do. Excellence, then, is not an act, but a habit.

— ARISTOTLE

Change your thoughts and you change your world.

— NORMAN VINCENT PEALE

The mind is everything. What you think, you become.

— BUDDHA

INTRODUCTION

Do you have any habits that you'd like to change? Or any troublesome fears that may be holding you back in the workplace, such as a fear of speaking up in a meeting?

You have come to the right place. Neurolinguistic programming is a well-established approach in psychology that produces positive changes in your desired behavior.

I am Elliott Middleton, PhD. My journey from a university professor specializing in finance and economics to an NLP aficionado began with a fascination with how our minds shape our realities. Having left academia, I served as a decision scientist for some of the largest financial institutions globally. I have witnessed firsthand the power of effective decision-making strategies and how important it is to program your mind to be adaptable and resilient.

This book is an up-to-date literature review on how to apply NLP in your life.

Neurolinguistic Programming began as a psychological theory in the 1970s, aiming to understand the connection between neurological processes, language, and behavioral patterns. It has since evolved, supported by scientific research, into a valuable tool for personal and professional growth. The essence of NLP lies in its ability to equip you with the means to reprogram your thought patterns, enhancing your life across multiple dimensions. While not every assertion made by NLP researchers has been successfully corroborated, there is no doubt that many practitioners of NLP have claimed to have benefitted greatly from it.

This book is crafted to guide you through understanding and applying NLP to achieve happiness and success. My approach intertwines scientific evidence with personal stories and practical exercises to provide a robust understanding of NLP. This isn't just about theory; it's about actionable change.

To you, the reader: I understand the hurdles you face daily —whether in climbing the career ladder, improving personal relationships, or overcoming personal barriers. This book is your toolkit to navigate these challenges and emerge victorious.

Structured and user-friendly, the book breaks down complex concepts into actionable insights and exercises. Each chapter builds on the previous one, ensuring an engaging, practical, cohesive learning experience.

I invite you to not just read but engage deeply with the content. Mastering NLP requires practice and consistency, but the results—enhanced communication, heightened self-awareness, and more effective decision-making—can redefine your sense of possibility.

Moreover, this book is just the beginning. To support your ongoing growth in NLP, access to a community and additional online resources will be available, ensuring you have the support needed to continue advancing your journey.

So, let's begin this journey together. Embrace the techniques, apply the insights, and join a community of learners stepping into a brighter, more prosperous future. Together, we can turn aspirations into achievements.

1

FOUNDATIONS OF NEUROLINGUISTIC PROGRAMMING

A seasoned executive steps up to the podium in the bustling conference room. Months ago, public speaking was her greatest fear, yet today, she commands the room with an undeniable presence. Her secret? A strategic application of Neurolinguistic Programming (NLP) techniques that reprogrammed her fears into powerful drivers of confidence. This profound transformation, a testament to NLP's transformative power, underscores its potential to bring about significant change in both professional and personal realms. Her story is not just about overcoming fear but about the empowering nature of NLP, inspiring hope and a sense of possibility in all who hear it.

1.1 What is Neurolinguistic Programming? An Introduction

Definition and Scope

Neurolinguistic Programming, or NLP, is a dynamic approach to communication, personal development, and psychotherapy formulated in the 1970s. It operates on the premise that there is a connection between neurological processes, language, and behavioral patterns learned through experience. NLP posits that these can be changed to achieve specific goals in life. Essentially, it provides tools and skills for modifying behavior and instilling new ways of thinking and feeling. Rooted deeply in the interplay between mind (neuro) and language (linguistic), NLP examines how their interaction affects our body and behavior (programming).

Core Objectives of NLP

The primary objectives of NLP are multifaceted, each focusing on enhancing the human experience. One core goal is the improvement of personal communication. NLP equips you to speak effectively, listen, and interpret others' communication with greater clarity and empathy. Enhancing personal development is another crucial objective; NLP techniques are designed to help you identify, refine, and achieve your personal and professional aspirations. Moreover, NLP is instrumental in assisting individuals to overcome psychological barriers, such as phobias, anxiety, and depression, often resulting in significant life changes.

Principles and Presuppositions

At the heart of NLP lie several foundational principles and presuppositions guiding its practice. One of the most pivotal is 'The map is not the territory,' a metaphor suggesting that individual perceptions of the world do not necessarily reflect the world itself. This principle helps individuals understand that their perspectives and reactions are based on their internal maps, which are subjective representations of reality, not on the absolute truth of reality. By recognizing this, individuals can open pathways to change and understand that their perceptions can be altered, leading to new choices and solutions. Another essential presupposition is 'Choice is better than no choice.' This principle emphasizes the value of flexibility in thinking and behavior. NLP encourages expanding these maps to perceive multiple choices in any situation, enhancing freedom and effectiveness in responding to life's challenges. It suggests that more options allow for better decision-making and problem-solving, leading to more favorable outcomes.

Real-World Applications

The versatility of NLP is evident in its broad utility across a diverse range of areas. In therapy, NLP techniques are used to treat psychological disorders and instill positive behavioral changes. In business, these techniques enhance leadership, improve teamwork, and boost sales performance by improving communication and negotiation skills. Educators use NLP to understand learning styles better, adapt teaching methods, and enhance student engagement. Additionally, NLP skills are employed in personal development for goal setting, increasing motivation, and building resilience. Each application demonstrates NLP's broad utility in transforming thoughts and behaviors and the outcomes of our personal and professional lives, equipping individuals with valuable tools for personal and professional growth, empowering them to take control of their lives and achieve their full potential.

Interactive Element: Reflection Section

Now, let's engage in a thought-provoking exercise. Consider your current challenges or goals. How might your perception of these be a reflection of your 'map' and not the 'territory'? Expanding your map to view these challenges from different perspectives might reveal new solutions and choices. How could you apply NLP principles to these challenges to achieve a different outcome? Take a moment to reflect on these questions and consider the potential of NLP in your life.

1.2 The History and Evolution of NLP: Key Figures and Milestones

Origins and Founders

The inception of Neurolinguistic Programming in the 1970s marked a pivotal shift in the therapeutic and personal development landscapes. Conceived by Richard Bandler, a psychology student, and John Grinder, a linguistics professor, NLP emerged from their intense study of the interplay between neurological processes and language patterns. Bandler and Grinder were particularly fascinated by the successful therapy techniques of gestalt therapist Fritz Perls, family therapist Virginia Satir, and hypnotherapist Milton Erickson. They observed these therapists and began to model their actions, analyzing their language and behavioral patterns. This modeling formed the foundational methodology of NLP—identifying and replicating successful individuals' language structures and behavioral patterns to achieve specific outcomes (Bandler & Grinder, 1975, 1976, 1979).

Evolution Over the Decades

Over the decades, NLP has evolved significantly in theory and application. From its roots in therapy, it has branched into myriad sectors, including business, education, sports, and even politics, adapting and expanding its techniques to meet the diverse needs of practitioners and clients. This adaptability reassures practitioners and clients of NLP's effectiveness, instilling confidence in its ability to address their specific needs. In the 1980s and 1990s, NLP gained considerable traction, with practitioners and scholars enhancing and refining the methodologies to include sensory-based interventions and communication strategies. This period also saw the development of numerous training programs and the establishment of institutions dedicated to teaching NLP to a broader audience. The adaptability of NLP principles has allowed their integration into various professional practices, contributing to its growth as a global phenomenon.

Influential Models and Theories

Among the most influential contributions to NLP is Virginia Satir's work, whose family therapy methods emphasized the importance of communication and the power of self-worth. Milton Erickson's hypnotic techniques also significantly shaped NLP's focus on the unconscious mind and its ability to influence conscious behavior, mainly through metaphor and storytelling. Gregory Bateson's theories on systems thinking and cybernetics provided a framework for understanding the interconnectedness of human behaviors and the environments in which they occur. These foundational theories have been instrumental in shaping NLP's approaches to understanding human behavior and facilitating change. They underscore the NLP premise that behavioral excellence can be modeled, learned, and transferred to others, providing powerful personal and professional growth strategies.

Current Status and Global Impact

Today, NLP is a recognized and practiced discipline globally, influencing countless individuals and organizations. Psychotherapists employ these techniques to help clients reframe their thoughts and overcome mental health challenges. In the corporate world, NLP enhances leadership skills, improves teamwork, and boosts sales performance. Educational professionals use NLP strategies to understand student behaviors and learning styles better, enhancing teaching methods and academic outcomes. The global impact of NLP is also evident in its broad cultural adaptability; it has been effectively applied in various cultural contexts, demonstrating its universal relevance and utility. NLP continues to evolve, driven by ongoing research and the innovative applications of practitioners worldwide. It solidifies its role as a valuable personal and professional development tool and inspires a sense of community among its global practitioners. The Annotated Bibliography provides many references with summaries showing the current scope of NLP.

1.3 Understanding the Building Blocks: Representational Systems

Neurolinguistic Programming (NLP) operates through what are known as representational systems, which are essentially the methods by which individuals perceive, store, and retrieve information from their surroundings using their senses. These systems are categorized primarily into visual, auditory, kinesthetic, olfactory, and gustatory modalities. People tend to have a preferred system or combination of systems they use more than others. For instance, a visual person might think in pictures and have a keen eye for detail in their environment, while an auditory person might focus more on sounds, tones, or words. Kinesthetic individuals are more in tune with bodily sensations or emotional feelings. Olfactory and gustatory systems, though less commonly discussed, focus on smells and tastes.

Identifying one's predominant representational system is crucial for enhancing self-awareness and improving interpersonal communication. By understanding your primary system, you can better comprehend how you process information and interact with the world, which in turn helps you to recognize and adapt to the preferred systems of others. For example, when you know you are primarily auditory but your colleague is visual, you might provide written documents or visual aids to support your verbal explanations during presentations. This not only improves the clarity of communication but also significantly enhances the rapport between individuals by aligning communication styles to meet the sensory preferences of others.

Matching and mirroring techniques in NLP are direct applications of this understanding. These techniques involve subtly matching or mirroring your communication partner's body language, tone, speed, and breathing patterns. By aligning your representational system with theirs, you create a subconscious sense of familiarity and trust, making the interactions smoother and more effective. This is particularly useful in negotiations, therapy sessions, or any setting where building a quick and deep rapport is beneficial.

To practically integrate the understanding of representational systems into your daily interactions, consider these exercises:

1. **Sensory Awareness Exercise:** Spend a day focusing on one particular sensory system. For example, choose the visual system and notice everything you see in vivid detail. The next day, switch to another sensory system, like auditory, and pay close attention to the sounds around you. This exercise will heighten your sensory understanding and help you become more aware of how you and others interact with the world.

2. **Feedback Gathering:** After a conversation or meeting, ask for feedback on how the information was received. Use questions like, "How clear was my explanation?" or "What could make my message clearer?" This will provide insights into your peers' representational systems and how you might better align your communication to their preferences.

3. **Matching and Mirroring Practice:** In your following conversation, consciously adopt the posture, gestures, voice tone, and speaking rate of your conversation partner. Note any changes in the flow of the interaction and the response from the person you are mirroring.

These exercises are designed to enhance your understanding of different sensory modalities and improve your flexibility in switching between them, depending on the context of the interaction and the preferences of those you are communicating with. This adaptability is critical to proficiently using NLP to enhance communication and build stronger relationships in both personal and professional contexts.

1.4 The Power of Linguistics: How Language Shapes Our Reality

Language is not merely a tool for communication but an influencer of our cognitive processes and behaviors. In the context of Neurolinguistic Programming (NLP), language is considered a pivotal lever for transformation. Every word and phrase we choose can shape our reality, influencing our thoughts and feelings and those of others around us. This linguistic influence is foundational in NLP, harnessing the subtle nuances of language to create shifts in perception and behavior that align with desired outcomes. For instance, simply reframing a challenge as an opportunity can dramatically alter one's emotional and physiological response, transforming a potential stressor into a catalyst for growth and innovation.

NLP emphasizes the critical role of language through the concept of linguistic presuppositions. These assumptions in our statements often go unnoticed but significantly shape our perceptions and behaviors. For example, when a manager says, "Can you try to complete this report by Monday?" the presupposition is that there might be room for failure or non-completion. On the other hand, stating, "Please complete this report by Monday," presupposes that the task is achievable and expected to be completed. By becoming aware of and strategically using presuppositions, you can influence outcomes and steer conversations in more constructive directions. This aspect of NLP teaches us that subtle shifts in language can lead to shifts in our interactive dynamics and self-perceived limitations.

The Meta-Model, a fundamental tool in NLP, serves as a linguistic compass to guide us toward more transparent communication and understanding. It is a model that helps to uncover the often hidden meanings in what people say. The Meta-Model challenges us to question and refine our language by breaking vague statements into specific, actionable information. For instance, if someone asserts, "I'm not good with people," the Meta-Model encourages a deeper inquiry, such as, "What specifically makes you believe you are not good with people?" This clarifies the statement and opens up pathways for change by identifying specific areas for improvement. The Meta-Model is particularly effective in therapy and coaching, where clarifying language helps to reveal underlying issues and misconceptions that keep individuals from achieving their potential.

Refining our language use is crucial in both personal and professional contexts. Techniques for language refinement in NLP involve actively listening, reflecting, and carefully choosing words that match the desired outcomes. One effective technique is the use of positive language to engage and motivate. For example, replacing negative commands such as "Don't forget" with positive alternatives like "Remember to" eliminates the presupposition of forgetting and actively encourages the desired behavior of remembering. Similarly, using inclusive language such as "We" instead of "You" can foster a sense of teamwork and shared responsibility, which is especially beneficial in collaborative professional environments.

Moreover, practicing precise language encourages us to avoid generalizations, deletions, and distortions in our speech. By articulating thoughts with clarity and precision, we reduce misunderstandings and increase the effectiveness of our communication. For leaders, educators, therapists, and individuals alike, mastering this aspect of NLP can lead to more influential and empowering interactions. As we refine our language, we become better communicators and more adept at navigating the complexities of human relationships and personal challenges. The linguistic strategies of NLP empower us to create a reality that resonates with our aspirations and values, proving that the pen—and the spoken word—is indeed mightier than the sword.

1.5 Programming the Mind: How NLP Works with Neurology

Neurolinguistic Programming (NLP) is not merely a psychological construct but is deeply rooted in neurological science. The basis of NLP's effectiveness lies in its ability to influence neural pathways directly—the network of neurons that dictate how we think, feel, and behave. When we practice NLP techniques, we essentially rewire these pathways, creating new neural connections that lead to lasting changes in our behavior and thought processes. This scientific underpinning is crucial in understanding how NLP facilitates transformation and why its effects are significant and enduring.

Neuroplasticity, the brain's ability to reorganize itself by forming new neural connections throughout life, is central to NLP's work. This ability means the brain is incredibly adaptable and can change its structure and function in response to new experiences, thoughts, and environments. By applying NLP techniques, we introduce new cognitive and behavioral patterns that the brain integrates into its neural architecture. This could mean replacing a fear response with a confidence response in certain situations or transforming a habit of procrastination into one of proactive action. Each time we practice an NLP technique, we strengthen these new neural pathways, gradually making them the brain's default pathways for reacting to similar situations in the future.

Anchoring is one of the most powerful NLP techniques for leveraging neuroplasticity. It involves creating a 'trigger'—such as a touch, a word, or a specific gesture—that evokes a particular mental state or emotion. For example, if you repeatedly listen to a specific song while feeling motivated, eventually, hearing that song will instantly evoke motivation. Anchors can be strategically placed to trigger positive states of mind that support success and well-being, such as calmness, focus, or joy. Effective anchoring helps manage emotional states and consolidates the desired states in the neural architecture, making it easier to activate these states when needed.

State management, another critical NLP technique, involves controlling your mental and emotional state rather than being controlled by it. It's about recognizing that while we cannot always control external events, we can manage our reactions by choosing our mental and emotional states. This technique relies on the understanding that our mental states are linked to our neurological states and that we can change our cognitive experience by changing our physiology and focus. Techniques such as breathing exercises, posture adjustments, and mental rehearsals shift and stabilize these states, promoting more adaptive and resourceful ways of interacting with the world.

The impact of these NLP interventions on neurological processes is not just theoretical but is evidenced in numerous case studies. One such case involved a senior executive who suffered from severe performance anxiety, which affected her ability to speak in public—a critical part of her role. Through a series of NLP sessions, specific anchors were created to trigger a state of calm and confidence immediately before and during her presentations. Additionally, she learned to maintain these states through state management techniques throughout her engagements. Neurological scans before and after the NLP interventions showed increased activity in the areas of her brain associated with calmness and confidence during public speaking. Over time, these state changes became more automatic, illustrating how NLP not only altered her psychological responses but also her brain's wiring.

These examples underscore the connection between NLP and neurological science. By understanding and applying the principles of neuroplasticity, anchoring, and state management, NLP practitioners can facilitate significant, lasting changes in themselves and their clients. These changes are not just about temporary improvements but fundamental shifts in how individuals experience and interact with the world, demonstrating the true power of NLP to reshape lives from the inside out.

1.6 Setting the Stage: Creating Your NLP Practice Environment

Essentials of an NLP Practice Space

Creating an effective NLP practice environment requires careful consideration of both the physical setup and the psychological atmosphere. The space where you engage in NLP should promote a sense of calm and concentration, free from distractions that might divert focus from the tasks at hand. Ideally, this space should be a dedicated area where privacy can be maintained, which is crucial for practicing techniques like self-hypnosis or deep relaxation without interruption. Lighting is also significant; natural light is preferable, but soft artificial lighting can create a soothing atmosphere. Including personal elements that inspire relaxation and positivity, such as plants, artwork, or personal mementos, can further enhance the space's ambiance, making the practice of NLP more enjoyable and effective.

Psychological preparation is equally important. This involves creating a mental space to escape the day's stresses and fully engage with NLP techniques. It can be helpful to begin each session with a few minutes of meditation or deep breathing exercises to clear the mind and establish a focus on personal growth. Setting clear intentions for what you wish to achieve during practice can also guide your activities and enhance the techniques' efficacy. Whether the goal is to improve communication skills, overcome a personal fear, or increase self-awareness, these intentions can direct your efforts more effectively.

Tools and Resources

Various carefully selected tools and resources can significantly enhance your NLP practice. Essential readings such as

"The Structure of Magic" by Richard Bandler and John Grinder (Bandler & Grinder, 1975, 1976), which lay foundational concepts and techniques of NLP, are invaluable. Audio recordings of guided NLP exercises complement these, and they are particularly useful for beginners needing clear, step-by-step guidance. Digital applications designed for NLP practitioners can also support practice, offering interactive sessions, tracking progress, and providing reminders for regular practice.

Additionally, visual aids such as charts that outline key NLP models and processes can serve as quick references during practice sessions. For more digitally inclined people, online platforms offer vast resources, including tutorials, video demonstrations, and webinars that can deepen understanding and introduce new techniques. These digital tools are handy for staying updated on the latest developments in NLP practice and theory.

Creating a Routine

Incorporating NLP into daily life necessitates a consistent routine for reinforcing new skills and behaviors. Establishing a specific time each day dedicated to NLP practice can help form a habit. This routine could involve various activities, including reading NLP material, practicing techniques such as anchoring or reframing, or listening to audio recordings. The key is consistency; even 15 to 20 minutes daily can lead to substantial progress over time.

For those looking to integrate NLP more deeply into their everyday lives, applying NLP techniques in real-world interactions and personal reflections can be beneficial. For example, consciously employing positive language patterns during conversations or practicing mental rehearsal before critical engagements can extend the benefits of NLP beyond structured practice sessions, making its principles second nature.

Community and Support

Engaging with a community of fellow NLP practitioners can

significantly enhance your learning experience. Community support provides motivation, diverse insights, and shared experiences that can deepen your understanding of NLP. Participating in forums, local meetups, or online groups can connect you with individuals ranging from novices to seasoned experts, each bringing valuable perspectives to discussions and problem-solving.

Workshops and seminars offer structured opportunities to learn from experienced NLP professionals and are invaluable for expanding their skills. These gatherings also provide a platform for networking, which can lead to collaborations and the formation of study groups that support ongoing learning. For those who prefer a more structured approach to community engagement, a mentorship arrangement with a more experienced practitioner can provide personalized guidance and feedback, which is particularly beneficial when navigating complex NLP concepts or techniques.

Your venture into NLP involves acquiring techniques and creating an environment that nurtures continuous growth and connection. The physical and psychological space you cultivate, the resources you choose, the routine you establish, and the community you engage with all play integral roles in your journey toward mastering NLP. Each element should align with your goals and learning style, ensuring your practice is effective and rewarding. Remember, the true power of NLP lies not just in the techniques themselves but in how they are integrated into your life to foster genuine and lasting change.

2

———

MASTERING SELF THROUGH NLP

I magine stepping into a bustling room filled with potential business partners. Where many might see intimidation, you see a canvas of opportunity. This is no mere fantasy; it's a tangible reality accessible through mastering the techniques of Neurolinguistic Programming (NLP), a psychological approach that involves understanding and influencing human behavior through language and other forms of communication. This chapter will examine the intricacies of silencing your inner critic, a crucial step towards unleashing your potential in personal and professional arenas (Dilts, Grinder, Bandler, & DeLozier, 1980).

2.1 Silencing the Inner Critic: Techniques to Overcome Negative Self-Talk

Understanding the Inner Critic

The 'inner critic' is that internal voice that whispers (or sometimes shouts) nothing but criticism and pessimism. Its origins are often rooted in early life experiences, societal expectations, and personal setbacks. This voice might tell you you need to be more intelligent, skilled, or deserving enough to achieve your goals. While its ostensible role might seem to be about protecting you from failure or embarrassment, more often than not, it sabotages your efforts, leading to decreased self-esteem and mental well-being. Recognizing that this voice is a common human experience rather than a personal flaw can be incredibly liberating, empowering you to take control of your narrative and life story.

Cognitive Restructuring Techniques

One effective method to combat the inner critic is cognitive restructuring, a core element of NLP that involves identifying and challenging destructive thought patterns such as 'I'm not good enough' or 'I always fail.' This technique encourages you to question the validity of the critic's harsh judgments and replace them with more constructive and realistic assessments. For instance, if your inner critic tells you you'll never succeed in your new business venture, cognitive restructuring would have you assess this belief critically: What evidence supports this notion? Have there been instances where you have succeeded in similar ventures? Often, you'll find that the critic's assertions are based on fear rather than fact. Reframing these thoughts can silence the critic and reduce its impact on your mental state.

Use of Positive Affirmations

Incorporating NLP-enhanced positive affirmations is another powerful strategy to counteract the effects of negative self-talk. NLP-enhanced positive affirmations are affirmations that are phrased in the present tense and embody achievable attributes, aligning with the principles of NLP. These are positive, empowering statements that, when repeated often, can help you reprogram your mind to believe in your capabilities and worth. For example, instead of saying, 'I will be confident,' affirm, 'I am confident in my abilities.' Regularly vocalizing these affirmations can fortify your mental resilience against the inner critic, gradually replacing doubt with a conviction in your self-worth.

Regular Practice and Reflection

The transformation from a negative to a positive internal dialogue takes time and effort. It requires consistent practice and reflection, which can be facilitated through daily journaling. Each day, dedicate a few minutes to write down any instances where the inner critic surfaced. Reflect on the situation: What triggered the criticism? How did you respond? Did you employ cognitive restructuring or affirmations? Over time, this practice not only diminishes the power of the inner critic but also strengthens your ability to replace negative thoughts with positive ones automatically. Remember, change is a process, not an event. Be patient with yourself and trust these techniques' power to bring about positive change.

Interactive Element: Reflection Section

This reflective exercise will further enhance your understanding and control over your inner critic. List three common criticisms your inner critic levies against you. Next to each, write a counter-statement using the cognitive restructuring technique. Repeat these counter-statements as affirmations daily. Monitor your feelings and beliefs over the next month, and note any changes in your journal. This exercise helps weaken the critic's grip and empowers you to advocate for your inherent worth and capabilities.

As you continue to engage with these techniques, remember that the goal is not to eradicate self-doubt but to manage it effectively. By doing so, you transform your inner dialogue into a supportive ally, propelling you towards personal and professional success. This mastery over your internal narrative is a crucial component of NLP, setting the stage for further growth as you continue exploring the subsequent techniques and strategies outlined in this chapter. It's okay to have moments of self-doubt; what matters is how you manage them and keep moving forward.

2.2 Building a Positive Self-Image with NLP

A robust self-image is a cornerstone of success in all facets of life; it shapes how we interact with the world, influences our relationships, and drives our professional achievements. When you perceive yourself positively, you emit confidence, which attracts positive responses from others. This reciprocal relationship between self-perception and external success is pivotal. For instance, consider a professional who views himself as a competent and valuable team member; this belief not only boosts his performance but also enhances the quality of interactions with colleagues, contributing to a more collaborative and productive work environment.

Neurolinguistic Programming offers powerful visualization techniques to fortify a positive self-image. In the context of NLP, visualization involves creating vivid, detailed mental images of the person you aspire to become. This practice leverages the brain's inability to distinguish between real and vividly imagined experiences. By frequently visualizing yourself succeeding in various scenarios—delivering a flawless presentation or navigating challenging negotiations—you begin to cement these competencies in your self-image.

Here's how to start: Find a quiet space, close your eyes, and picture yourself in a desired situation. See yourself performing at your best, observe the positive reactions of others, and feel the emotions associated with this success. Repeat this exercise daily, ideally in the morning or right before bed, to reinforce these positive images and make them an integral part of your self-concept.

Aligning your self-image with your personal and career goals is another application of NLP. This alignment ensures that self-perception supports and enhances your journey towards these objectives. NLP modeling techniques are invaluable here; they involve identifying and emulating the qualities and behaviors of someone who already excels in the areas related to your goals. Choose a role model whose achievements and attributes resonate with your aspirations. Study their behavior, mindset, and how they respond to challenges. Integrate these observations into your self-image by adapting their successful strategies as your own. For instance, if your goal is to become more influential within your professional network, you might model your interactions on a respected leader known for their compelling communication skills and strategic thinking.

Creating positive feedback loops through behavioral changes is crucial in reinforcing and sustaining a new, positive self-image. A feedback loop refers to the process where positive behaviors reinforce the self-image, and a strong self-image promotes further positive behaviors, creating a cycle of continuous improvement. To establish such a loop, start by setting small, achievable goals that reflect your new self-image. No matter how minor, each accomplishment provides tangible proof of your capabilities, reinforcing your self-image. Regularly acknowledge these successes and use them to propel yourself toward larger goals. This practice solidifies your self-image and builds resilience, making it easier to maintain positivity in the face of future challenges.

By integrating these NLP techniques into your routine, you foster a self-image that reflects your true potential and propels you towards realizing it in every walk of life. Whether enhancing personal relationships, achieving professional success, or navigating the complexities of daily interactions, a positive self-image serves as your steadfast ally. This empowered self-perception becomes deeply ingrained through consistent practice, guiding you toward a fulfilling and successful life.

2.3 Boosting Self-Esteem through Effective Anchoring Techniques

Anchoring in Neurolinguistic Programming (NLP) is a powerful technique that involves creating a stimulus-response association to evoke particular emotional states. This concept, derived from the classical conditioning theory proposed by

Ivan Pavlov, can be strategically used to trigger positive emotional states such as confidence, calmness, or joy. Understanding anchoring basics involves recognizing that specific sensory experiences can trigger our emotional responses—be it a touch, a sound, or a visual cue. For instance, the smell of a particular perfume might instantly remind you of a comforting moment in your childhood, eliciting feelings of safety and warmth. In NLP, you can deliberately create such associations to bring beneficial emotional states when needed.

Creating personal anchors involves identifying a specific, reproducible trigger and deliberately associating it with a peak emotional state. To establish an anchor, identify a situation where you feel a strong positive emotion. This could be a moment of achievement, a peaceful memory, or any situation where you felt particularly empowered. As you relive this memory, engage all your senses to intensify the experience—notice what you see, hear, and feel. At the peak of this emotional state, introduce a unique sensory trigger. This could be a specific hand gesture, a touch on a particular body part, or a unique verbal phrase. This trigger mustn't be something you commonly encounter in daily life; it should be distinct enough to maintain its association with the positive state. With repetition, this trigger will become your anchor, capable of eliciting the desired emotion whenever you activate it.

Maintaining and adjusting anchors over time is essential as your emotional landscape and life circumstances evolve. An anchor that once evoked confidence might lose its effectiveness if overused or associated with a different context where the outcome could have been more favorable. To maintain the potency of your anchors, revisit and reinforce them periodically in contexts where they are likely to induce the desired outcome. Additionally, be prepared to adjust your anchors by changing the sensory trigger or the emotional state it is linked to, ensuring they remain aligned with your current goals and needs. This might mean updating the context in which you activate the anchor or creating new anchors for different purposes as your personal and professional landscapes change.

Several real-world scenarios demonstrate the successful application of anchoring to enhance self-esteem. Consider the case of a sales professional who struggled with anxiety during client presentations. By establishing an anchor associated with feelings of calm and confidence—triggered by pressing her thumb and forefinger together—she delivered her pitches with newfound poise and assurance. Each successful presentation reinforced the anchor, making it more robust and reliable. Another example involves a young athlete who used a visual anchor—a specific image on his wristband—that he associated with peak performance states during practice. Viewing this image during competitions helped trigger the mental and physical states conducive to optimal performance, significantly improving his results.

Through these examples, it's evident that anchoring can be a beneficial tool in NLP, offering a method to control and utilize emotional states to bolster self-esteem and achieve personal excellence. By understanding and applying this technique, you equip yourself with a mechanism to instantly access resourceful states, enhancing your ability to handle challenges more effectively and confidently. This skill boosts self-esteem and empowers you to navigate situations with assurance and agility. As you continue to explore and integrate anchoring into your life, the benefits will manifest in heightened self-esteem and improved overall well-being and success.

2.4 Utilizing Submodalities to Enhance Self-Perception

In Neurolinguistic Programming (NLP), submodalities refer to the fine distinctions we make about our sensory representations—essentially, how we experience our perceptions through sight, sound, touch, taste, and smell. These subtle cues within each sensory modality can significantly influence the intensity and quality of our experiences. For instance, visual submodalities include brightness, distance, and color, while auditory submodalities might involve tone, volume, and tempo. Understanding and adjusting these submodalities can dramatically alter our emotional responses to memories or anticipated future events, offering a powerful tool for enhancing self-perception and emotional health.

The capacity to change perceptions using submodalities is one of NLP's most dynamic features. You can change your feelings about it by altering the submodalities associated with a particular memory or future worry. For example, consider a distressing memory that continues to affect your confidence. By imagining this memory in black and white instead of color or visualizing it much smaller and further away, its emotional impact can be significantly lessened. Similarly, modifying the submodalities of a future event that causes anxiety—such as imagining a calm and slow speech instead of a nervous and quick one—can reduce stress and improve performance.

To effectively utilize submodalities to enhance self-perception, you can perform specific exercises designed to practice these adjustments. Select a memory or future scenario that elicits a strong emotional response. Visualize this scene in your mind, paying close attention to the current submodalities. Now, begin to adjust these submodalities one by one. Play with the color, size, and distance if it's a visual memory. If it involves sound, modify the volume or tone. Notice how each change affects your emotional response to the memory or anticipated event. This exercise not only helps in managing emotional responses but also empowers you to take control of how external events impact your inner peace and self-image.

The long-term benefits of mastering submodality adjustments can be significant. Regular practice can improve mental health as you develop the ability to quickly and effectively alter the emotional valence of your thoughts and memories. This skill is valuable in combating persistent negative thoughts, reducing undue stress, and overcoming limiting beliefs hindering personal and professional growth. Moreover, enhanced control over your emotional responses leads to greater resilience, allowing you to face life's challenges with a more balanced and composed mindset. Over time, as you become adept at submodality manipulation, you'll find that your overall perception of life becomes more positive and empowered, reflecting a self-image that supports and enhances your capacity to achieve your goals and fulfill your potential.

2.5 The Swish Pattern: Transforming Undesirable Behaviors

The Swish Pattern is a dynamic and effective technique within Neurolinguistic Programming that aims to modify undesirable behaviors that hinder personal and professional growth. This method replaces an unwanted image or behavior with a desired one, using a rapid, swishing action in the mind's eye. Its purpose is to disrupt the old behavior pattern and anchor in a new, more empowering behavior. By repeatedly practicing the Swish Pattern, you can condition your mind to automatically activate positive responses in situations that previously triggered negative behaviors.

A clear understanding and meticulous approach are essential to utilize the Swish Pattern effectively. Identify a specific behavior you wish to change, such as hesitating during public speaking. Visualize this behavior vividly as if you are watching a scene from a movie, noting all the details that accompany the hesitation—perhaps your stance, the audience's faces, and the feelings of doubt creeping in. This image will serve as your cue image.' Next, create a 'replacement image,' which depicts you performing the desired behavior, such as speaking confidently, engaging with the audience, and feeling empowered. Make this image bright, colorful, and filled with positive emotions.

Now, for the transformation process: in your mind's eye, see the cue image and, in one swift motion, have it shrink rapidly to a point and disappear, immediately replaced by the replacement image exploding into full-size, vibrant, and compelling. This 'swish' should be rapid and executed with energy. Practice this swish—around five to ten times—each time, ensuring the replacement image becomes more apparent and the positive feelings more substantial. Common pitfalls during this practice include not being specific about the behaviors or making the swish too slow. The key is rapid, decisive action in your visualization, which symbolically casts away the old behavior and firmly establishes the new one.

Integrating the Swish Pattern into daily life requires consistent practice and mindfulness. Begin by setting aside a few minutes each day to practice the technique, ideally at a time when you are relaxed and free from distractions. As you become more proficient, start to apply the Swish Pattern in real-time situations. For instance, mentally perform the swish to activate the desired behavior if you notice the trigger for your old behavior. Over time, this practice will embed the new behavior more deeply, making it your natural response.

The efficacy of the Swish Pattern is not merely anecdotal; numerous success stories attest to its power. One notable example involves a young professional who struggled with procrastination, which affected his career progression. By applying the Swish Pattern, he replaced the image of himself delaying work with an image of tackling tasks energetically and efficiently. This simple mental shift significantly improved his productivity and job performance, leading to a much-anticipated promotion. Another success story comes from a woman who used the Swish Pattern to overcome her fear of flying, a phobia that had restricted her personally and professionally. By replacing her fear with images of herself enjoying flights, she could travel overseas for a critical business meeting, which she aced, thanks to her newfound confidence.

These stories highlight the Swish Pattern as a method for behavior change and a catalyst for broader life transformations. By mastering this technique, you equip yourself with a powerful tool to reshape not just minor habits but pivotal elements of your behavior that influence significant life outcomes. As you continue to apply and adapt the Swish Pattern to various aspects of your life, you'll find its benefits permeating deeper, enhancing your ability to respond to life's challenges with agility and confidence.

2.6 Creating Personal Empowerment: A Step-by-Step Guide

Personal empowerment in the context of Neurolinguistic Programming (NLP) is fundamentally about gaining control over your own life. It's about setting goals that resonate deeply with your values and beliefs and systematically working towards achieving them with purpose and self-efficacy. Empowerment through NLP is not just about harnessing techniques to modify behaviors or enhance communication; it's about cultivating an inner strength that propels you toward your aspirations, enabling you to navigate challenges with resilience and confidence. This sense of empowerment is crucial because it affects every aspect of your life—from your relationships and career to your mental and physical health.

To foster personal empowerment, NLP provides strategies that can transform your approach to life. One pivotal strategy is goal setting, which in NLP is not just about defining what you want to achieve but aligning these goals with your deeper psychological needs and values. This alignment ensures that your pursuits are energizing rather than draining, contributing to a sustainable drive and focus. Another powerful NLP strategy is role modeling, which involves identifying and emulating the qualities and behaviors of individuals who embody the success you seek. This strategy leverages the principle of 'modeling' in NLP, which posits that the capabilities that allow someone to be successful can be replicated. By observing and integrating these traits, you enhance your skills and bolster your belief in your ability to succeed.

Building a personal empowerment plan is a dynamic process that should start with a transparent and honest assessment of your current state. Evaluate your strengths, weaknesses, opportunities, and threats in a structured manner. This assessment will serve as the foundation of your empowerment plan. Next, clearly define your short-term and long-term goals, ensuring they are specific, measurable, achievable, relevant, and time-bound (SMART). Incorporate NLP techniques such as visualization to enhance your emotional and psychological connection to these goals; visualize the achievement of these goals and the process of working towards them. Visualization strengthens your commitment and motivation, making your goals more tangible and attainable.

Moreover, your empowerment plan should include strategies for developing and refining skills necessary for your goals. This might involve enhancing your communication skills, learning new professional skills, or improving emotional intelligence. Each skill area should have specific actions, resources, or activities to help acquire or enhance skills. This could include workshops, books, online courses, or even NLP sessions focusing on specific competencies.

Monitoring and adapting your empowerment plan is crucial to ensure it remains relevant and responsive to your evolving needs and circumstances. Regular progress reviews are essential; these should be as frequent as monthly or quarterly. During these reviews, assess what is working and what isn't and make adjustments where necessary. This might involve setting new goals, removing ones that no longer serve you, or finding different strategies for achieving existing goals. Challenges and obstacles are inevitable, but with a flexible and adaptive plan, they become opportunities for learning and growth rather than roadblocks.

Building and refining your empowerment plan is about achieving goals and developing a deeper understanding of yourself and your capabilities. It's about transforming the narrative of your life so that you are not just reacting to circumstances but actively creating the life you desire. As you implement and refine your plan, you will notice a significant boost in your confidence and greater control over your life's direction.

Empowerment is a continuous journey, and as you progress through these steps, you are building a robust framework for personal success and satisfaction. Each step brings you closer to your goals and reinforces your capability to navigate future challenges with greater agility and assurance. As you conclude this chapter and move forward, carry with you the understanding that true empowerment comes from within. Consistent efforts and an unwavering commitment to personal growth and excellence nurture it. The techniques and strategies outlined here are tools to help you on this path, providing you with the means to unlock your full potential and achieve both success and a sense of fulfillment and purpose.

3

ACHIEVING PROFESSIONAL
EXCELLENCE

In the fast-paced world of modern business, the line between a leader and a follower often hinges on skills, knowledge, and the ability to connect, persuade, and lead with conviction. Imagine the potential to transform every professional interaction into a catalyst for growth and impact. This isn't just a lofty goal but a tangible reality when you leverage the power of Neurolinguistic Programming (NLP) in leadership. This chapter is a journey into the realm of NLP, showcasing how it can empower you, as a leader, to enhance your leadership capabilities, focusing on building rapport, influence, and a revolutionary approach to leading others.

3.1 NLP for Effective Leadership: Building Rapport and Influence

Understanding Leadership Dynamics

Leadership transcends the essential act of management to encompass a deeper connection with team members and stakeholders. It requires a blend of emotional intelligence and the ability to establish rapport, which are critical in fostering trust and motivation. Emotional intelligence in leadership involves understanding and managing your emotions and those of others to enhance interpersonal dynamics and decision-making. Rapport, the close and harmonious relationship in which the people or groups concerned understand each other's feelings or ideas and communicate smoothly, is the bridge that connects a leader's vision with their team's execution.

NLP enhances these aspects by providing tools that align leaders' emotional responses with their leadership goals, improving their ability to connect with and influence their teams. For instance, by learning to read and match the emotional states of team members, leaders can more effectively address concerns, inspire effort, and navigate conflicts. This emotional alignment makes communication more effective and ensures leaders are heard, understood, and respected.

Techniques for Building Rapport

Building rapport is an art that can be systematically enhanced with NLP techniques. Two key strategies in NLP are mirroring and matching. Mirroring involves subtly copying the body language, speech patterns, or attitudes of the person you are communicating with. This does not mean mimicking, which is obvious and potentially offensive, but subtly reflecting movements and postures. For example, if a team member is calm and soft-spoken, adopting a similar tone can create a sense of similarity and comfort in the interaction.

Matching extends beyond physical and verbal cues to include matching values, priorities, and even breathing patterns. By aligning yourself with what matters to your team, you demonstrate empathy and understanding, cornerstones of effective leadership. This doesn't mean compromising your values but finding common ground that enhances mutual respect and cooperation.

Influencing Techniques

Influencing in leadership should be subtle and, importantly, ethically grounded. NLP equips leaders with powerful influencing techniques, such as presuppositions and embedded commands. Presuppositions are assumptions implicit in communication. For instance, by stating, "When you complete this project successfully," you presuppose that success is expected and achievable. Embedded commands are directives embedded within a larger sentence, which can subconsciously guide team members' thoughts. For example, "Consider how you might approach this task innovatively" embeds the command 'approach this task innovatively' within a seemingly casual suggestion. When used judiciously, these techniques enhance a leader's ability to guide and motivate their team subtly and effectively, ensuring that the leadership message is delivered and acted upon ethically and respectfully.

When used judiciously, these techniques enhance a leader's ability to guide and motivate their team subtly and effectively, ensuring that the leadership message is delivered and acted upon. However, it's crucial to note that these techniques should be used cautiously and always ethically. Misuse of NLP techniques can lead to manipulation and damage trust and relationships within the team. Therefore, consistently applying these techniques with respect and integrity is essential.

Case Studies on Leadership Transformation

Real-world applications of NLP in leadership abound. Consider the case of a tech company CEO who struggled with high staff turnover. He significantly improved team morale and retention rates by applying NLP techniques to understand underlying team dynamics and improve communication. He used mirroring and matching during individual meetings to better connect with employees, addressing their needs and concerns genuinely and reassuringly.

Another example involves a nonprofit leader who used presuppositions effectively to secure funding and support for new initiatives; by framing her proposals around when, not if, the funding would be secured, she instilled confidence and expectation in her stakeholders, which played a crucial role in the successful expansion of her organization's impact. These are just a few examples of how NLP techniques can be applied in leadership scenarios, and there are many more ways to use these techniques to enhance your leadership skills.

These cases are a testament to NLP's potential. They illustrate how NLP can reshape personal leadership styles and elevate entire organizations' collective efficacy and morale. Integrating NLP strategies into your leadership approach opens new avenues for connection, influence, and success. This potential for transformation should fill you with hope and optimism for the future of your leadership journey. However, it's important to remember that mastering these techniques takes practice and feedback. By consistently applying these techniques and seeking input from your team, you can refine your skills and make every leadership interaction more effective and impactful.

3.2 Advanced Language Patterns for Perspective Communication

Exploring the depths of the Milton Model unveils a fascinating vista on hypnotic communication, particularly its utility in business contexts. Originating from the therapeutic techniques of Milton H. Erickson, this model is a cornerstone in the study of Neuro-Linguistic Programming, emphasizing the power of language to influence subconscious processing. The Milton Model employs artfully vague and metaphorically rich language to encourage the listener to fill in gaps with their experiences, facilitating deeper personal connections to the message. This approach can be beneficial in professional settings, allowing leaders and communicators to bypass resistance and foster a collaborative atmosphere.

The structure of the Milton Model is intricately designed to weave a web of subtle and impactful suggestions. It utilizes patterns such as indirect suggestions, which, unlike direct commands, do not trigger resistance because they are often perceived as less invasive and more acceptable. For instance, instead of saying, "You need to improve your sales technique," a Milton Model approach might involve saying, "Imagine how successful you could be if you discovered new sales techniques." This method of communication invites the listener to envision a possibility and, in doing so, subtly guides them toward the desired behavior without direct insistence.

Crafting persuasive messages using specific NLP language patterns involves a keen understanding of the nuances of verbal cues and the underlying psychology of persuasion. Effective persuasive communication in a business environment often requires conveying information and inspiring action and commitment. Utilizing embedded commands within your dialogue is a strategic way to achieve this. An embedded command, such as "Consider the benefits this project will bring," can be particularly persuasive as it subtly suggests taking action without making demands, thereby maintaining a positive interaction dynamic.

Moreover, using analogies and metaphors can also enrich the persuasive quality of communications. These figures of speech make the information more relatable and memorable, help bridge different perspectives, and enhance understanding. For example, comparing a business strategy to steering a ship through a storm can vividly encapsulate the challenges and skills involved in navigating a business through difficult market conditions. By crafting messages that resonate on multiple levels, you can effectively engage your audience, making your communications heard, felt, and remembered.

Strategies for overcoming resistance in negotiations and discussions are essential for any business professional. Resistance often stems from fear, misunderstanding, or a lack of trust, and overcoming it requires a strategic and empathetic approach. Pacing and leading, a core technique in NLP, is instrumental. Pacing involves acknowledging the current reality of the situation or the other person's viewpoint, thereby building rapport and trust. Following this, leading, where you gradually introduce new ideas or perspectives, can be implemented. For instance, in a negotiation, you might start by agreeing with the other party's concerns (pacing), then gradually introduce your proposal as a solution to these concerns (leading).

Pacing and leading should be complemented with effective listening and reframing techniques. Listening actively to the concerns and needs of others provides valuable insights into their perspectives and demonstrates respect and openness. Reframing involves changing the context or perspective of a problem or a situation. For instance, if cost is a significant concern in a negotiation, reframing it as an investment in quality or long-term savings can shift the perspective and reduce resistance.

Practical Exercises to Enhance Persuasive Communication Skills

To refine your persuasive communication skills, consider engaging in the following exercises designed to apply the principles discussed:

1. **Embedded Command Practice:** Create a list of directives you commonly use in professional interactions. Rewrite these as embedded commands. For example, change "You should join our meeting tomorrow to discuss this further" to "Imagine the insights you could gain by joining our discussion tomorrow." Use these revamped phrases in your communications and observe the responses you receive.

2. **Metaphor Development:** Identify a key idea or concept you often need to communicate in your work context. Develop three different metaphors to

convey this idea. For instance, if the concept is about overcoming business challenges, you might use metaphors related to sports, weather, or historical events. Test these metaphors in your presentations or meetings to see which resonates most with your audience.

3. **Pacing and Leading Exercise:** In your following conversation, practice pacing by mirroring the other person's speech rate, tone, and language. Once you feel rapport is established, attempt to lead by introducing new ideas or suggestions aligned with the conversation's flow. Reflect on how effectively you could shift the conversation and note any adjustments needed for future interactions.

These exercises enhance your ability to communicate persuasively and deepen your understanding of how language influences thought and action in professional settings. By integrating these advanced NLP techniques, you equip yourself with a powerful toolkit for effective and impactful communication, paving the way for tremendous success and influence in your professional endeavors.

3.3 Goal Setting for Career Success Using NLP Techniques

Setting clear, actionable, and resonant goals has never been more critical in a landscape where career trajectories are no longer linear but dynamic. SMART goals—Specific, Measurable, Achievable, Relevant, and Time-bound—have long served as a cornerstone in effective goal-setting frameworks. Yet, within Neurolinguistic Programming, these parameters are not just guidelines but gateways to deeper, more intrinsic values that align with your personal and professional growth. SMART goals structured through the lens of NLP become achievable and motivating as they are imbued with personal significance and clarity.

To transform standard SMART goals into tools of extraordinary change, one must infuse them with compelling emotional and psychological depth, a process where NLP excels. For instance, consider a goal to "increase sales by 20% in the next quarter." To align this with NLP principles, reflect upon the specific emotional states that achieving this goal will produce. How will success feel? What does it mean for you personally and professionally? By associating detailed sensory experiences and positive emotional states with this goal, you engage the subconscious mind—a powerful ally in achieving targeted outcomes. This sensory-rich goal setting clarifies what success looks like and enhances the intrinsic motivation to pursue it by making it resonate personally.

Further enriching the goal-setting process is the use of NLP visualization techniques. Visualization is not merely about seeing the result but involves immersing yourself in the experience of achieving your goals. This practice should be vivid and detailed, encompassing all senses. If your goal consists of delivering a successful pitch to a potential client, visualize not only the act of presenting but also the setting, the reactions of your audience, the questions they might ask, and the feeling of satisfaction and confidence as you respond adeptly. This visualization solidifies your psychological and emotional alignment with the goal, enhancing focus and performance. It transforms the abstract into the tangible, making the path to achievement more transparent and the outcome more attainable.

Aligning personal goals with your organization's broader missions and values is critical in ensuring career success. This alignment ensures that your professional efforts contribute to larger corporate objectives, which can lead to greater job satisfaction, recognition, and advancement opportunities. You must first understand your organization's core values and strategic objectives to achieve this. Engage with leadership, review company materials, and reflect on how your role contributes to the bigger picture. Then, craft your goals to advance your aspirations and push the company's agenda forward. This harmonization increases your value within the organization and deepens your engagement and commitment to your work as your successes resonate with more prominent achievements.

Tracking and adjusting your goals is crucial in maintaining their relevance and effectiveness. The use of NLP feedback loops is instrumental in this process. A feedback loop in NLP involves observing the results of your actions, learning from them, and then adjusting your behaviors and strategies accordingly. Implementing this involves regular reviews of your goal progress, ideally with input from mentors or supervisors who can provide external perspectives and insights. During these reviews, ask yourself: Are my strategies effective? What have I learned from the successes and setbacks? How can I adjust my actions to better align with my goals? This reflective practice ensures that your goals remain aligned with your changing professional landscape and personal growth and reinforces the NLP principle of flexibility in pursuit of excellence.

Incorporating these NLP techniques into your goal-setting and achievement strategies transforms the process from a routine administrative task into a dynamic, personalized growth plan. By setting goals that are not only SMART but also emotionally and personally resonant, visualizing success in rich detail, aligning personal aspirations with organizational values, and maintaining agility through regular feedback and adjustments, you equip yourself with a robust framework for sustained professional success and personal fulfillment.

3.4 Managing Workplace Stress Through NLP Strategies

In the modern workplace, stress is as much a part of the environment as computers and conference rooms. Yet, not all stress is detrimental if managed effectively. It can propel you toward deadlines and fuel your drive to overcome challenges. However, when stress becomes chronic, it can hinder performance, decrease job satisfaction, and impact your overall health. Thus, identifying and managing stress through tailored Neurolinguistic Programming (NLP) techniques can transform potentially harmful situations into opportunities for personal growth and resilience.

The first step in managing workplace stress effectively is to identify its sources, which can be as varied as the tasks on your daily to-do list. Workplace stress triggers often include looming deadlines, high expectations, interpersonal conflicts, or a lack of control over your work. Personal stressors might also spill over into your professional environment, compounding your pressure. Recognizing these triggers is crucial; it involves a keen awareness of the situations or interactions that elevate your stress levels. Keep a stress journal for a week or two, noting the daily occurrences that generate stress. This record will help you pinpoint patterns and specific triggers, laying the groundwork for effective NLP interventions.

Once you've identified these stress triggers, NLP offers powerful techniques for managing and reducing them. Reframing and dissociation are particularly effective. Reframing involves changing your perspective on a stress-inducing situation to view it in a more positive or manageable light. For instance, if the thought of a big presentation causes anxiety, reframe it: instead of seeing it as a threat, view it as a chance to showcase your knowledge and contribute to your team's success. This shift in perspective can reduce anxiety and enhance your performance. Dissociation, another NLP technique, involves mentally stepping back from a stressful situation to view it with objective detachment. Imagine watching the stressful situation as if it were a scene in a movie, including yourself as a character. This technique can help reduce the immediacy of the stress, allowing you to react more calmly and thoughtfully.

Building a resilient mindset is another cornerstone of effective stress management. Resilience in the workplace means being able to bounce back from setbacks and adapt to challenging conditions flexibly. NLP fosters resilience by enhancing your internal dialogue—the ongoing conversation with yourself. By consciously shifting this dialogue from critical to supportive, you reinforce your ability to face and overcome workplace challenges. Techniques such as positive affirmations and visualization play a crucial role here. Regularly visualizing yourself handling stressful situations with competence and calm can reinforce your self-image as a resilient person, making you more likely to react as such in real situations.

Incorporating routine NLP practices into your daily work life can help maintain low stress levels. Start each day with a grounding NLP exercise, such as a visualization or a few minutes of deep breathing with positive affirmations. For example, before beginning work, close your eyes and deeply inhale, envision calmness entering your body, and exhale stress. Pair this with affirmations like, "I handle my work calmly and effectively." Such practices can center your mind and prepare you to face the day's stresses more serenely. Additionally, setting regular intervals to assess your mind throughout the day can help catch and address rising stress levels before they become overwhelming. Techniques like the 'swish' pattern can be used in these moments to quickly switch from stress to calm.

Understanding and applying these NLP strategies transforms your approach to workplace stress from reactive to proactive. This enhances your immediate work environment and improves your long-term career success and personal well-being. Embracing these techniques equips you with the tools to navigate the complexities of modern professional life with greater ease and confidence, turning potential stress into a pathway for growth and achievement.

3.5 NLP Techniques for Conflict Resolution

In any professional setting, conflict is inevitable. It arises from differences in opinions, goals, and personal values among team members or between employees and management. Understanding the dynamics of workplace conflicts is crucial in addressing them effectively. Typically, these conflicts stem from miscommunications, misaligned objectives, or competition for limited resources. However, beneath these surface causes, perception plays a pivotal role. How individuals perceive each other's actions and intentions can significantly influence the escalation or resolution of conflict. For example, if one team member perceives another's insistence on quality as nitpicking rather than a shared commitment to excellence, it can lead to friction and resentment.

Reframing techniques are invaluable in shifting these perceptions and changing the narrative around conflicts. Reframing involves altering the context or perspective from which a situation is viewed. Reframing can transform a contentious issue into an opportunity for collaborative problem-solving in conflict situations. For instance, if two departments are in conflict over resource allocation, reframing the situation to highlight the mutual goal of organizational success can shift the focus from competition to collaboration. This technique encourages parties to view the problem through a lens of shared objectives rather than opposing agendas, fostering a more constructive dialogue.

Mediation using NLP techniques can resolve conflicts by facilitating effective communication between conflicting parties. Effective mediation requires the mediator to remain neutral, helping each party express their views without bias. NLP techniques such as pacing, leading, and active listening are crucial here. Through pacing, the mediator acknowledges and reflects each party's feelings and viewpoints, creating a rapport and a safe space for open communication. Subsequently, leading can be gently introduced to guide the parties towards mutual understanding and compromise. For instance, after acknowledging a team member's frustration with workload distribution, a mediator might lead by suggesting ways to discuss possible adjustments that could benefit both the individual and the team.

Preventive strategies are equally important in managing workplace conflicts. These strategies involve proactive measures to prevent conflicts from arising or escalating. One effective preventive strategy is anticipatory communication adjustments. This approach consists of adjusting communication strategies based on anticipating potential disputes. For example, if a manager knows that two team members have historically clashed over project approaches, proactively clarifying roles and expectations before project commencement can prevent misunderstanding. Additionally, establishing regular feedback sessions where team members can voice concerns and suggestions in a structured manner can prevent minor grievances from escalating into major conflicts.

By applying these NLP techniques, you can transform conflict resolution from a reactive to a proactive skill. Instead of merely responding to conflicts as they arise, you become adept at recognizing potential triggers, understanding the underlying dynamics, and employing strategies that resolve disputes and enhance team cohesion and communication. This proactive approach to conflict resolution minimizes disruption and contributes to a healthier, more collaborative workplace environment. Each conflict resolved through these techniques becomes a stepping stone toward building a stronger, more resilient team capable of navigating challenges with greater ease and confidence.

3.6 Enhancing Presentation Skills Through NLP

Presentations are a critical aspect of professional communication, whether you are pitching an idea, sharing quarterly results, or delivering a keynote at a conference. The effectiveness of a presentation often hinges not just on the content but also on the presenter's ability to connect with the audience and convey the message confidently and clearly. Neurolinguistic Programming (NLP) offers techniques to elevate your presentation skills by enhancing confidence, engaging your audience, and ensuring your message is heard and remembered.

Building Confidence with Anchoring

One of the most immediate challenges in presentations is managing nervousness and exuding confidence. As mentioned, NLP tackles this through anchoring techniques, which involve creating and activating a trigger to evoke a desired emotional state. To establish an anchor for confidence, begin by recalling a moment when you felt exceptionally confident and successful. Immerse yourself in that memory, relive the sensations, and at the peak of those feelings, establish a physical gesture, such as touching your thumb and forefinger together. This gesture becomes your anchor, which you can activate before and during your presentation to create confidence. Practicing this technique regularly can make the response more automatic and robust, giving you a reliable boost whenever you speak.

Engaging the Audience

The effectiveness of your presentation is also determined by how well you connect and engage with your audience. This requires understanding how people process information, known as representational systems in NLP. Some people respond more to visual information, others to auditory details, and others to kinesthetic (feeling-based) cues. To engage all these types, use a mix of visuals (like slides or graphs), storytelling (to capture auditory learners), and questions or prompts that encourage the audience to think or feel personally connected to the content. Observing audience reactions during the presentation can also guide you in real-time adjusting your approach, ensuring maximum engagement across all representational systems.

Using Metaphors and Stories

Metaphors and storytelling are powerful tools in NLP that can make your presentation impactful and memorable. Metaphors link the unfamiliar with the familiar, helping the audience understand complex ideas through more straightforward, relatable concepts. Incorporating stories, especially those with emotional undertones, can significantly enhance retention and empathy. When preparing your presentation, weave in relevant stories or analogies that align with your key points. This not only aids in keeping the audience engaged but also helps them remember the information long after the presentation ends.

Feedback and Improvement

Continuous improvement is vital to mastering presentation skills. NLP suggests using feedback constructively to refine your approach. After every presentation, seek input from diverse sources. Ask specific questions beyond whether they liked the session; inquire about what resonated most, what was unclear, and how the presentation could be more engaging. Use this feedback to identify patterns and areas for improvement.

Additionally, self-reflection is crucial. Consider recording your presentations to review your performance. Pay attention to your body language and how well you keep the audience engaged. This self-assessment and external feedback will provide a comprehensive basis for continually enhancing your presentation skills.

Applying these NLP techniques transforms the art of presentation from a routine task into an impactful communication experience. By anchoring confidence, engaging diverse audiences, utilizing metaphors, and integrating feedback, your presentations become more than just information delivery—they become memorable, influential experiences that can propel your professional effectiveness and reputation.

Reflect on the power of NLP in enhancing presentation skills—a crucial toolset for any professional looking to influence and inspire. The techniques discussed here are strategies and pathways to deeper connections with your audience, ensuring your messages are delivered and resonate deeply. As you continue to apply and refine these skills, they become integral components of your professional repertoire, enhancing your presentations and broader communication skills. In the next chapter, we will explore further applications of NLP in professional settings, expanding your toolkit for success and influence in all your business interactions.

4

———

NLP FOR EMOTIONAL AND PSYCHOLOGICAL WELL-BEING

Imagine stepping into a serene landscape, untouched by the chaos of everyday life, a place where each breath restores peace and balance to your mind. This visualization isn't just a temporary escape but a glimpse into the possibilities when you master the art of emotional regulation through Neurolinguistic Programming (NLP). In this chapter, we describe practical NLP techniques that equip you to navigate the complexities of emotions, transforming potential turmoil into a state of emotional equilibrium and intelligence.

4.1 Emotional Regulation with NLP: Techniques and Practices

Understanding Emotional Triggers

The cornerstone of mastering emotional regulation is identifying your emotional triggers—specific situations, words, or actions that elicit strong emotional responses. These triggers, often rooted in past experiences, could be situations where you feel undervalued, words that remind you of a traumatic event, or actions that make you feel rejected. Their recognition is crucial for effective emotional control. For instance, if criticism from colleagues consistently sparks undue anger or anxiety, this reaction might be traced back to early experiences of feeling undervalued or dismissed. Other examples of emotional triggers could be a fear of failure, rejection, or public speaking. By mapping out these triggers, you can understand the underlying patterns of your emotional responses. This awareness is the first line of defense, allowing you to anticipate and prepare for potential challenges, thus minimizing their disruptive impact.

Use of Anchoring for Emotional Stability

Anchoring is the foundational NLP technique for inducing emotional stability. Regularly activating this anchor in safe environments can strengthen its effectiveness, making it a reliable resource during challenging times.

Swish Pattern for Emotional Control

The Swish Pattern is a powerful NLP technique for transforming negative emotional responses into more positive or neutral ones. It involves mentally replacing a negative image or thought with a positive one, thereby changing your emotional reaction. You can apply this technique to situations that trigger negative emotions, such as a fear of heights, a past traumatic event, or a stressful work situation. Practicing this exercise while in a safe space can help rewire your neural pathways, reducing the intensity of the adverse reaction and reinforcing the positive response.

Routine Practices for Emotional Regulation

Consistent practice is critical to making NLP techniques effective tools for emotional regulation. Daily exercises can help integrate these strategies into your life, enhancing your emotional intelligence. Begin each morning with a five-minute anchoring session to set a positive tone for the day. Throughout the day, be mindful of emotional triggers and employ the Swish Pattern to maintain emotional control. Additionally, end your day by reflecting on your emotional challenges and how effectively you managed them, considering adjustments for future encounters. Over time, these practices enhance your ability to regulate your emotions and contribute to a deeper understanding and mastery of your emotional landscape. This emphasis on daily practice encourages commitment and engagement in your self-improvement journey.

Interactive Element: Emotion Tracking Journal

To further enhance your emotional regulation skills, maintain an Emotion Tracking Journal. Daily entries should include instances where emotional triggers were activated, the techniques used to manage your responses, and the effectiveness of these techniques. This journal is a practical tool for observing patterns in your emotional reactions and tracking your progress in managing them. Regular reviews of this journal can offer insights into the most effective strategies for your emotional regulation, guiding ongoing adjustments and improvements in your approach.

Integrating these NLP techniques into your daily routine transforms your emotional regulation approach from reactive to proactive. This shift enhances your well-being and empowers you to navigate life's challenges with greater ease and resilience. As you continue to explore and apply these strategies, the art of emotional regulation becomes a cornerstone of your psychological well-being, enabling you to maintain balance and tranquility amidst the complexities of life.

4.2 Overcoming Anxiety with NLP: A Practical Approach

Anxiety, a familiar unwelcome guest for many, can often make you feel like you're living in a constant state of 'what-ifs.' Understanding and managing your anxiety isn't just about quelling temporary fears but about developing a deep, intuitive understanding of your emotional patterns. Neurolinguistic Programming (NLP) offers tools that not only allow you to chart these patterns but also empower you to reshape your relationship with anxiety, putting you in the driver's seat of your emotional well-being.

The first step in this process involves mapping out your anxiety patterns. This means observing and noting when and where you typically feel anxious, what thoughts are associated with these feelings, and how you physically and emotionally react. Identifying these patterns can often reveal the triggers that set off your anxiety, which may be specific situations, ongoing stresses, or even recurring thoughts that bring about a physiological response.

Once these patterns are clear, NLP techniques empower you to interrupt them, offering a new pathway to calm. For instance, if you notice that your anxiety often surfaces during meetings at work, you might pinpoint the fear of being judged or making a mistake as an underlying trigger. With this awareness, you can begin to apply targeted NLP strategies to mitigate these triggers before they escalate into full-blown anxiety. This proactive approach not only lessens the immediate symptoms of stress but also gradually diminishes the power these triggers have over your emotional state, leading to more sustained periods of calm and confidence. This gradual reduction of anxiety triggers offers hope and optimism about your progress in managing anxiety, showing that change is possible and within reach.

Reframing anxious thoughts is another powerful technique in NLP that can be particularly effective in altering the internal narrative that fuels anxiety. Reframing involves changing your perspective on the anxiety-inducing thoughts to lessen their impact. For example, suppose the thought, "I'm going to ruin this presentation and disappoint everyone," tends to initiate a spiral of anxiety. In that case, you might reframe it to, "I'm fully prepared for this presentation and ready to share my knowledge." This shift doesn't deny the presence of nervousness but changes the narrative from one of impending doom to one of preparedness and potential success. By continuously practicing this technique, you can replace negative anticipations with more positive and supportive ones, significantly reducing the anxiety they produce.

Dissociation is another valuable tool in managing anxiety. This technique involves mentally stepping back from the anxiety-inducing situation to observe it from an emotionally detached perspective. Imagine watching yourself in the anxiety-triggering situation as if you were a neutral observer or seeing it play out on a movie screen. This perspective can reduce the immediacy and emotional impact of the problem, allowing you to assess it more rationally and respond more calmly. Dissociation can be particularly useful in acute moments of anxiety, providing a mental 'breathing space' to regain composure and perspective.

Building a comprehensive personal anxiety management plan involves integrating these NLP techniques into a consistent, practical framework tailored to your needs. Start by establishing a routine incorporating daily NLP practices such as morning affirmations or visualizations promoting calm and confidence. Regularly engage in mapping and reframing exercises to keep a check on your anxiety triggers and modify your responses to them. Include techniques like dissociation and anchoring in your plan to manage acute anxiety episodes effectively. Additionally, setting aside time for regular review and adjustment of your plan is crucial. This ensures that the strategies you are using remain effective and responsive to your evolving relationship with anxiety.

By committing to this structured approach, you empower yourself with the tools to manage anxiety and transform your overall emotional resilience. Over time, these practices can help you develop a more relaxed and confident demeanor, not just in previously anxiety-inducing situations but across all areas of your life.

4.3 NLP Strategies for Coping with Depression

Depression often weaves a complex web of negative

thoughts and patterns that can overshadow one's life, making even everyday tasks seem impossible. Recognizing and understanding these patterns are crucial steps in combating depressive symptoms. These patterns may manifest as persistent sadness, loss of interest in enjoyable activities, or a pervasive sense of worthlessness. Such thoughts are not just fleeting sadness but persistent whispers that color your perception of the world and yourself. Identifying these patterns involves keen self-observation and reflection. You might notice, for example, that your depression deepens during periods of stress or isolation or that specific thoughts consistently precede your darkest moods. By mapping these patterns, you gain the initial power to predict and preempt the grips of depression, setting the stage for effective intervention.

Intervention techniques in NLP provide tools to disrupt depressive thought patterns and replace them with healthier, more constructive ways of thinking. One powerful technique is the use of counteracting affirmations. When you catch yourself spiraling into negative thoughts, intentionally inject positive affirmations that are specific and believable. For instance, if a common depressive thought is "I never do anything right," counter it with, "I have succeeded in many aspects before, and I can succeed again." These affirmations must be rooted in personal truth to be effective. Over time, this practice can help weaken the hold of negative patterns and reinforce a more positive mental landscape.

Another NLP technique involves the use of symbolic representation. This involves personifying depression as an external entity, which can then be interacted with and managed more objectively. Visualize and dialogue with this entity, asking why it's there and what it needs to leave. This externalization helps to detach your identity from the depression, allowing you to deal with it as a separate, manageable aspect rather than an overwhelming part of your existence. This technique not only lessens the emotional weight of depressive feelings but also empowers you to reclaim control over your mental state.

Creating compelling futures is another cornerstone of the NLP strategy for dealing with depression. This technique leverages the power of visualization to foster hope and motivation, which are often eroded in depressive states. Begin by envisioning a future where you have overcome depression, focusing on the details of this new reality. What are you doing differently? How do you feel? What have you achieved? Visualizing these scenarios in vivid detail can create a mental and emotional blueprint that motivates action toward these futures. This practice provides a temporary escape from current struggles and plants the seeds for sustained change, making a happier life seem attainable and real.

Routine and structure play pivotal roles in managing depression, providing a framework that counters the chaos and unpredictability of depressive moods. Establishing a daily routine that includes specific times for waking up, meals, exercise, work or study, and relaxation can help impose order and predictability, which are soothing to a troubled mind. Moreover, integrating regular NLP practices into this routine can enhance its effectiveness. For example, set aside time each morning for a visualization exercise focusing on positive outcomes or practice mindfulness meditation before bed to calm the mind and improve sleep quality. The consistency of these practices fosters a sense of normalcy and control and reinforces the use of NLP techniques as tools for everyday emotional regulation.

By adopting these NLP strategies, you create a robust framework for combating depression. This approach doesn't just manage symptoms but also addresses the root patterns and thoughts that fuel depressive states, paving the way for an enduring recovery. As you continue to apply these techniques, the journey from darkness to light becomes increasingly filled with moments of clarity and empowerment, each step forward a testament to your resilience and the power of NLP.

4.4 Healing from Past Traumas Using NLP Therapies

Trauma can deeply engrain itself in our psyche, often influencing our thoughts, behaviors, and overall mental health in ways we might not fully realize. Neurolinguistic Programming (NLP) offers techniques for addressing and healing from these past traumas, transforming them from sources of pain into catalysts for growth and resilience.

One such technique is Timeline Therapy, which allows you to revisit traumatic events in a safe and structured manner. This therapy is based on the understanding that our memories are not just records of past events but are also influenced by our emotions and perceptions at the time of the event. Timeline Therapy involves visualizing a literal timeline on which you can 'travel' back to past experiences. The safety of this approach lies in its detachment—you revisit these memories not as a participant but as an observer, which can significantly reduce the emotional charge associated with the memory. During this process, you are guided to understand and reprocess the event, extracting lessons and releasing negative emotions like fear, guilt, or anger that may have been trapped since the occurrence.

By altering the emotional context of these memories, Timeline Therapy facilitates a shift in how these events affect your present and future life. For instance, if you have been holding onto guilt from a past mistake, revisiting this event through Timeline Therapy can help you forgive yourself and understand that this mistake does not define your worth or capabilities. This therapeutic journey is not about changing the past; it's about changing the past's hold over you, empowering you to move forward with greater freedom and self-compassion.

Changing the narrative surrounding a trauma is another crucial step in healing. This involves reshaping your story about what happened and why, turning it into a narrative of survival and growth rather than victimhood and suffering. This is where NLP techniques such as reframing come into play. Reframing allows you to view your traumatic experiences from different perspectives, highlighting your strengths and resilience. For example, instead of viewing a past failure incident as a mark of incompetence, you can reframe it to focus on your courage to try and the skills you gained through the experience. This shift in narrative can impact your self-esteem and outlook on life, reinforcing a view of yourself as a resilient individual who can learn and grow from all experiences, not just the positive ones.

Using Meta-Model questions in NLP can be particularly effective in aiding the healing process. These questions are designed to challenge and clarify the language we use to describe our trauma, uncovering the underlying beliefs that can keep us locked in patterns of negative thinking. For instance, if you often think, "I always mess things up," a Meta-Model question might be, "Have there been no instances where you succeeded?" This prompts a more accurate recall of past events, challenging the absolutism and negativity bias that trauma can instill. You open the door to a more balanced and positive self-perception by dissecting and questioning these ingrained beliefs.

Finally, the role of support systems cannot be overstated in the process of healing from trauma. NLP emphasizes building and maintaining strong support networks through friends, family, therapists, or support groups. These networks provide emotional comfort, validation, accountability, and perspective that can be crucial during healing. NLP techniques can strengthen these relationships by improving communication skills, enhancing empathy, and helping you clearly articulate your needs and boundaries. Regular interaction with a supportive community can provide continuous feedback and reinforcement, allowing you to remain committed to your healing journey and preventing backsliding into negative patterns.

Through these NLP therapies, you can approach your past traumas not as insurmountable obstacles but as opportunities for personal development. By safely revisiting traumatic events, reshaping your narrative of them, challenging limiting beliefs, and leaning on a supportive community, you equip yourself with the tools to not only recover from past wounds but also to thrive in the aftermath, embracing a future defined by resilience, growth, and emotional freedom.

4.5 Cultivating Happiness and Contentment through NLP

Cultivating enduring happiness and deep-seated contentment is a journey that extends beyond the surface of temporary pleasures and achievements. Through the strategic application of Neurolinguistic Programming (NLP), you can harness gratitude and positive framing to elevate your everyday experiences and anchor a lasting sense of joy and satisfaction. Practicing gratitude, an exercise within NLP, involves regularly acknowledging and appreciating the positive aspects of your life, both big and small. This practice shifts your focus from what is lacking or problematic to what is abundant and suitable. For instance, a gratitude journal listing three things you are grateful for daily can significantly shift your mental focus from deficit to abundance. Over time, this shift fosters a more optimistic and appreciative mindset, reducing stress and enhancing overall well-being.

Positive framing is another crucial technique in NLP that involves consciously reframing your perspective on life events to highlight potential benefits and learning opportunities rather than losses or obstacles. For example, viewing a job loss not as a setback but as an opportunity to pursue new career paths or passions can transform a challenging life event into a catalyst for personal growth and development. This technique mitigates the emotional impact of adverse events and empowers you to navigate life's ups and downs with resilience and proactive positivity. Regularly practicing gratitude and positive framing, you cultivate a mental environment where happiness and contentment can flourish, supported by a foundation of positive thoughts and perceptions.

Enhancing life's pleasures through NLP involves focusing on the submodalities of your sensory experiences. Submodalities, the specific qualities of how we perceive our experiences, can be finely tuned to intensify the pleasure derived from everyday moments. For example, if enjoying a quiet morning coffee is a cherished routine, focus on amplifying the experience's sensory details: the coffee's aroma, the cup's warmth in your hands, and the quiet ambiance of your environment. By adjusting these submodalities—making the aroma richer in your mind or visualizing the steam rising more vividly—you heighten the sensory pleasure of the moment. This practice can be applied to various aspects of life, from savoring meals to appreciating nature, effectively enhancing the quality and enjoyment of your daily experiences. Through regular practice, these enhanced moments build up a reservoir of positive emotions, contributing significantly to your overall contentment and well-being.

Aligning your life goals with your deepest values is another strategy in NLP that ensures your pursuits and achievements are successful and fulfilling. This alignment process involves deep introspection to identify your core values—what you consider important and meaningful in life. Once these values are clear, the next step is to evaluate your goals to ensure they resonate with them. For instance, if one of your core values is community service, aligning your career goals to include aspects of philanthropy or community engagement can significantly enhance your sense of personal fulfillment and happiness. This congruence between your goals and values ensures that your achievements bring not just success in conventional terms but also a sense of satisfaction and purpose, enriching your life experience significantly.

The role of community in personal happiness cannot be overstated. Humans are inherently social beings, and our connections with others are crucial to our overall well-being. NLP can enhance these social bonds and your engagement with your community through improved communication skills, empathy, and rapport building. You are actively participating in community activities, whether volunteering, joining clubs, or attending social events, which provides opportunities to connect with others who share your interests or values. These interactions enrich your social life and reinforce your sense of belonging and purpose within a more extensive social network. Moreover, NLP techniques can resolve conflicts and build stronger relationships within these communities, ensuring your social interactions are frequent, deeply satisfying, and supportive. By investing in and nurturing these social connections, you create a supportive network that enhances your happiness and provides a safety net during challenging times, making community engagement a vital component of a contented, fulfilling life.

Through these strategies, NLP offers a robust framework for achieving and enjoying success and happiness in life. By focusing on gratitude, anchoring your emotional state, enhancing sensory experiences, aligning goals with personal values, and fostering community connections, you lay down a multifaceted foundation for deep, lasting contentment. These practices, woven seamlessly into your daily life, ensure that your journey toward happiness is as rewarding as the destinations you aspire to reach.

4.6 Mastering Your Emotional States with NLP

Mastering your emotional states using Neurolinguistic Programming (NLP) involves a deep understanding of effectively managing and transforming your emotional experiences. NLP provides a robust toolkit for this purpose, including techniques for state elicitation and state change essential for anyone looking to enhance their emotional agility. State elicitation involves intentionally bringing forth a desired emotional state using NLP techniques. This might include recalling a memory that naturally evokes the desired emotion or using specific sensory cues like music or images to trigger the state. For instance, if you need to elicit a state of calm before a high-stakes meeting, you might visualize a tranquil beach scene, focusing on the details—the sound of the waves, the warmth of the sand, the smell of the ocean air—to help transport your emotions to a more serene place.

On the other hand, state change techniques are used when you find yourself in an undesired emotional state and need to shift to a more useful one. This might involve practices like the 'state to resource' switch, where you identify a resourceful state that will help you cope with your current situation more effectively. For example, if you feel overwhelmed by a project, you might switch to a state of curiosity about what you can learn from the task or gratitude for the skills you develop through this challenge. This shift alters your emotional state and perspective on the situation, enabling a more productive and positive engagement with the task.

Harnessing the power of physiology is another critical aspect of managing emotional states. It's well-documented in NLP that physiological changes can significantly influence your emotions. Simple adjustments to your posture, breathing, or facial expressions can immediately affect your feelings. For example, a posture of confidence—standing tall, shoulders back, chest open—can make you feel more confident. Similarly, controlled breathing techniques can help calm anxiety, while smiling can help elevate your mood. By becoming aware of these physiological cues and learning to manipulate them consciously, you gain a powerful tool for maintaining emotional control in various situations.

Consistency in practicing these techniques is crucial for achieving mastery over your emotions. Just as you would train regularly to improve your physical strength or learn a new language, regular practice of NLP techniques is essential for deepening your emotional intelligence and agility. This might involve daily practices such as morning visualization exercises, regular check-ins with yourself throughout the day to monitor and adjust your emotional state, or setting aside time each week to reflect on your emotional patterns and progress. Consistency helps reinforce these techniques until they become second nature and builds confidence in your ability to handle emotional challenges effectively.

Real-life applications of these NLP techniques abound, demonstrating their effectiveness in diverse scenarios. Consider the case of a healthcare professional who used state management techniques to handle the emotional toll of her job. By practicing state elicitation each morning, she cultivated compassion and resilience that supported her through her daily interactions with patients. Another example is a public speaker who used physiological techniques to overcome stage fright. By adopting power poses and controlled breathing before his speeches, he significantly reduced his anxiety and improved his performance.

These case studies illustrate the practical application of NLP techniques in managing emotional states and highlight their potential to impact personal and professional life. Whether enhancing job performance, improving interpersonal relationships, or simply leading a more balanced and fulfilling life, mastering emotional states through NLP offers significant benefits.

The journey to emotional intelligence is both challenging and rewarding. The techniques discussed provide a path to greater self-awareness and control, enabling you to navigate life's ups and downs with grace and resilience. The next chapter will build on these foundations as we move forward, exploring advanced NLP strategies for personal and professional growth. This continuation will deepen your understanding of NLP and expand your toolkit for achieving and sustaining peak performance in all areas of life.

PLEASE SHARE

If you have found value in this book, please share your experience by leaving a rating or review on Amazon. The algorithm rules at Amazon, and your review will enable more people to find this book.

If you are reading an ebook, please click this link to be taken to your review page.

If you are reading a print book, point your phone's camera at the QR code below to be taken to your review page. Thank you!

5

ENHANCING INTERPERSONAL RELATIONSHIPS

Imagine you are at a crucial networking event. Around you are potential contacts whose partnerships could catapult your career to new heights, yet engaging in meaningful conversations seems daunting. Here, the art of listening, not just hearing, becomes your most powerful tool. Mastering this skill can transform casual exchanges into valuable connections, making every interaction an opportunity to advance professionally and personally. This chapter focuses on honing your listening skills through Neurolinguistic Programming (NLP) techniques, ensuring you hear, truly understand, and connect with those around you.

5.1 The Art of Effective Listening: NLP Techniques

Understanding Active Listening

Active listening is a skill that transcends the mere act of hearing the words spoken by others. It involves fully concentrating on the speaker, understanding their message, responding thoughtfully, and remembering shared information. This form of listening is crucial in fostering deep, meaningful personal and professional relationships. It allows you to process the words and the complete message being communicated. This could include emotional undertones, hidden messages, and implicit calls to action, all vital for effective communication. By engaging in active listening, you demonstrate respect and interest in the speaker, enhancing trust and facilitating a deeper connection.

NLP Techniques for Better Listening

Neurolinguistic Programming offers tools that significantly enhance your listening skills. Techniques such as 'pacing' and 'leading' are theoretical concepts and practical skills you can apply in daily interactions. For instance, in a professional meeting, you can pace your speech to match the calm and composed tone of the speaker, creating a subtle rapport. This synchronization helps break down barriers and makes the speaker feel understood and valued. Once pacing is established, you can move to leading, which guides the conversation to deeper engagement or toward desired outcomes. For instance, by slowly altering your speech pattern from fast to a more thoughtful, slower tempo, you can also lead the speaker to slow down, making the conversation more deliberate and reflective.

Listening Beyond Words

To truly master the art of listening, it is essential to tune into more than just words. NLP teaches you to listen for subtext —the underlying messages or emotions that are not directly expressed. This involves paying close attention to non-verbal cues such as body language, facial expressions, and tone of voice, which can provide significant insights into the speaker's thoughts and feelings. Additionally, using Meta-Model questions can be incredibly powerful in clarifying any vagueness in communication. These questions are designed to probe deeper and encourage specificity; for example, if someone says, "I'm upset about the meeting," you might ask, "What specifically about the meeting upset you?" This not only shows that you are listening but also that you care enough to understand fully.

Practice Scenarios and Role Plays

Engaging in practice scenarios and role-play exercises can be highly beneficial to develop and refine your listening skills. Consider setting up practice sessions with a colleague or friend where you can role-play various conversational scenarios. One person could be the speaker discussing a recent challenge while the other practices active listening techniques. After the exercise, provide each other with feedback on the listening and communication strategies used. What was missed? What could be interpreted differently? These practice sessions are invaluable for honing your ability to listen deeply and respond appropriately, enhancing your interpersonal interactions across all areas of life.

Interactive Element: Listening Journal

Consider keeping a listening journal as a practical tool to enhance your listening skills. This journal is where you can reflect on your conversations and interactions, noting key points and your understanding of the speaker's message. After each significant conversation, take a few moments to jot down key points from the discussion. Reflect on how well you felt you understood the speaker and note any areas where you missed important subtext or non-verbal cues. Over time, review your entries to assess how your listening skills have improved and identify any consistent challenges you might need to address. This exercise reinforces your listening practice and encourages mindfulness in your communication.

However, it's important to note that incorporating these NLP techniques into your daily interactions can be challenging at first. It may take time and practice to master these skills, and you may encounter resistance or misunderstandings from others. But with dedication and practice, you can overcome these challenges and transform how you connect with others. A better listener improves interpersonal relationships and opens doors to more significant personal and professional opportunities. As you continue to practice and refine these skills, you'll find that your ability to understand and influence your social and professional environments will expand dramatically, paving the way for increased success and fulfillment in all areas of your life. This transformation is not just theoretical but a practical reality you can achieve with dedication and practice.

5.2 Building Deep Rapport with NLP

Rapport is the bridge that connects two individuals through streams of empathy, trust, and mutual respect. It is the foundation upon which all successful interpersonal relationships are built, whether in professional settings, personal encounters, or casual interactions. At its core, rapport creates a connection that transcends superficial interactions, enabling deeper communication and understanding. Empathy plays a pivotal role here; it involves genuinely understanding and sharing another person's feelings, which fosters a strong bond. Trust, another cornerstone of rapport, is built through consistent, reliable actions and transparent communication. Mutual respect involves acknowledging and valuing each person's differences, creating a nurturing environment where ideas and feelings can flow freely. These elements combined create a robust framework for developing meaningful connections that can significantly enhance personal and professional life.

To cultivate such connections, NLP offers specific techniques that can be immediately applied to improve your ability to build rapport. One of the most effective techniques is matching and mirroring, which involves subtly copying the body language, speech patterns, and even breathing rhythms of the person you are interacting with. This does not mean mimicking, an overt and often unwelcome replication of another's behaviors. Instead, it is a subtle, respectful alignment of your behaviors with those of another, creating a subliminal sense of familiarity and comfort. For instance, if you notice that the person you are speaking with uses gestures frequently, incorporating similar gestures into your communication style can make the conversation feel more natural and engaging for them. Similarly, matching the tone and volume of your voice to theirs can make them feel more heard and understood, deepening the connection.

Advancing beyond essential matching and mirroring, NLP also explores deeper strategies for rapport-building, such as synchronizing breathing patterns and sharing personal experiences. Breathing is intimately connected to emotional states; by aligning your breathing with another person, you can often synchronize emotional states, facilitating a deeper connection. This technique is beneficial in tense or emotional situations where calming the conversation can lead to more productive outcomes. Sharing personal experiences, especially those that relate to the experiences or feelings of the other person, can also significantly deepen rapport. It demonstrates empathy and an openness to vulnerability that can encourage the other person to open up and share more freely, further strengthening the bond.

Assessing the level of rapport in any relationship is crucial, as it allows you to adjust your communication strategies to better align with the interaction dynamics. NLP teaches several methods to gauge rapport, including observing verbal and non-verbal communication congruence. When people are in solid rapport, their body language, words, and breathing patterns tend to mirror each other. Another indicator is the level of comfort and openness in the conversation; high rapport typically leads to more fluid and expansive interactions. Notice signs of discomfort or disengagement, such as crossed arms, lack of eye contact, or short responses. These can be cues to adjust your approach by slowing the conversation, asking open-ended questions, or giving the person more space to express themselves.

Building and assessing rapport can be enhanced through role-playing exercises that simulate different social interactions. For example, you could practice with a colleague or friend, taking turns being the initiator of a conversation where the goal is to build rapport using NLP techniques. After the exercise, discuss what worked and what didn't, focusing on how well you could match and mirror behaviors, adapt your communication style, and, ultimately, establish a connection. These exercises improve your ability to build rapport and sharpen your observational skills and adaptability, which are essential components in relationship-building.

5.3 NLP for Better Family Dynamics

In the intricate dance of family life, communication patterns play a pivotal role in shaping relationships and dynamics within the household. These patterns, whether open and supportive or more closed and challenging, significantly influence the home's emotional climate. For instance, a family that frequently engages in clear, respectful communication will likely experience stronger bonds and fewer conflicts. Conversely, a household where communication is often unclear or confrontational might struggle with misunderstandings and tension. Recognizing these patterns is the first step in applying NLP techniques to enhance familial interactions. You can identify areas where changes could be beneficial by analyzing how family members communicate, including their chosen words, tone, body language, and response styles.

Applying NLP within the family setting involves adapting its principles to suit more intimate, emotionally charged relationships. One effective strategy is reframing, which consists of changing the context or perspective of a thought, idea, or situation to give it a more positive or empowering meaning. For example, a child's reluctance to participate in family chores could be reframed from a perspective of laziness to needing more engagement or understanding of the importance of contribution to family life. This changes how family members view and respond to the situation. Positive enforcement is another powerful tool, reinforcing positive behaviors through praise or rewards and encouraging their recurrence. This approach shifts focus from what's going wrong to what's going right, fostering a more positive and supportive environment.

Dealing with conflicts effectively is crucial in maintaining a healthy family dynamic. NLP offers several techniques that can be particularly useful in these scenarios. One such technique is perceptual positions, which encourages family members to view the conflict from different perspectives, including their own, the other person's, and a neutral third party's. This exercise fosters empathy and understanding, often leading to acceptable resolutions for all parties involved. Using Meta-Model questions in family discussions can help clarify meanings, reveal underlying issues, and reduce generalizations that usually exacerbate family conflicts. These questions probe deeper into statements made during disputes, helping to uncover the root of the problem and facilitating a more straightforward path to resolution.

Creating and maintaining a positive family environment is one of the most rewarding applications of NLP within the family context. This involves setting a tone of open communication where each member feels heard, valued, and respected. Techniques such as anchoring can establish a sense of calm and safety within the home. Family members can, for example, create a physical space where everyone feels comfortable discussing their feelings without judgment. Regular family meetings can serve as a platform for discussing issues, celebrating achievements, planning fun activities, strengthening bonds, and fostering a supportive atmosphere. The consistent application of these strategies improves day-to-day interactions and builds a foundation of trust and mutual respect that can support the family through any challenges.

By integrating NLP techniques into your family dynamics, you not only enhance communication and resolve conflicts more effectively but also contribute to a nurturing environment that supports the growth and well-being of each family member. As you apply these strategies, observe the shifts in your family's interactions and the overall emotional climate. Over time, you'll likely find these changes bring about a more harmonious and connected family life, rich with understanding and mutual respect.

5.4 Enhancing Romantic Relationships through NLP

Applying Neurolinguistic Programming (NLP) in romantic relationships can significantly enhance the depth and quality of connections between partners. A fundamental aspect of nurturing a fulfilling romantic relationship is deepening emotional ties, the bedrock for enduring companionship. Through NLP, couples can explore and establish shared values and goals critical for harmonious coexistence. Establishing shared values involves engaging in open discussions where both partners articulate their core beliefs and what they envision for their future together. This process not only clarifies expectations but also fosters mutual respect and understanding. Financial planning, family planning, or personal development goals should be set collaboratively. NLP techniques such as visualizing future outcomes can help both partners vividly imagine achieving these goals, enhancing commitment and partnership unity.

Deepening emotional connections also involves acknowledging and validating each other's emotional experiences. NLP's concept of emotional anchoring can be particularly beneficial here. Partners can create positive emotional anchors for each other by consistently associating their interactions with positive feelings and reassurances. For example, a simple gesture like a reassuring hand squeeze during a stressful moment can become an anchor, reminding the partner of the support and security within the relationship. Over time, these anchors strengthen the emotional foundation of the relationship, ensuring that both partners feel valued and understood.

Verbal and non-verbal communication is another pillar of relationship health that NLP can optimize. Effective communication in romantic settings is about speaking openly and ensuring both partners feel heard and understood. NLP offers several strategies to enhance this aspect. Using clean language —simple but specific phrases that avoid assumptions and judgments—can help express needs and desires without triggering defensiveness or misunderstanding. Non-verbal communication can be refined through synchronizing body language and voice tonality, making interactions more engaging and empathetic. For instance, mirroring your partner's posture or matching their tone can subconsciously create a sense of alignment and agreement, making conversations flow more smoothly.

Maintaining the health of a romantic relationship over the long term requires continuous effort and adaptability, which NLP facilitates through techniques such as periodic relationship check-ins and flexibility strategies. Regular check-ins, where partners dedicate time to discuss the state of their relationship, can help preemptively address potential issues and reaffirm their commitment to each other. These sessions provide a platform for both partners to express any concerns and appreciate positive developments in their relationship. NLP's flexibility strategies, which involve being open to adjusting one's behavior or perspective in response to changing dynamics, are crucial during life transitions such as career changes, parenthood, or relocation. By maintaining a flexible approach, partners can support each other through changes, strengthening their bond.

Addressing and overcoming typical relationship challenges such as jealousy or communication breakdowns requires a nuanced understanding of the underlying issues that NLP can provide. Jealousy often stems from insecurities or past traumas and can be mitigated through techniques that promote self-esteem and trust. For example, using NLP visualization techniques, a person can reconstruct their self-image into one that is confident and secure, reducing feelings of jealousy. Communication breakdowns can be resolved through conflict resolution strategies that involve recognizing and respecting each other's communication styles. Employing NLP's Meta-Model can uncover the root causes of misunderstandings by challenging vague expressions and clarifying intentions, leading to a more effective resolution of conflicts.

Applying NLP techniques within romantic relationships offers a pathway to a deeper connection, improved communication, and enduring partnership. By continuously applying these strategies, couples can navigate the complexities of their journey together, fostering a relationship that survives and thrives on mutual understanding, respect, and love.

5.5 Navigating Social Settings with Confidence: NLP Approaches

Navigating through the maze of social interactions, from casual gatherings to professional networking events, can often seem daunting. Yet, the ability to move through these with confidence and ease can open doors to invaluable opportunities. Here, Neurolinguistic Programming (NLP) becomes an essential tool, offering strategies to boost your social confidence and enhance your ability to adapt and thrive in various social contexts.

One fundamental aspect of building social confidence with NLP involves managing anxiety, which often acts as the most significant barrier to effective social interaction. Techniques such as anchoring can play a crucial role here. By creating a 'confidence anchor'—a physical gesture linked to feelings of confidence and calmness—you can invoke a confident state whenever needed. For instance, pressing your thumb and forefinger together while recalling a moment when you felt exceptionally confident can help establish this anchor. Over time, triggering this gesture in social settings can help you rapidly reclaim those feelings of confidence.

Additionally, visualization techniques empower you to rehearse successful social interactions mentally. Before attending a social event, you might visualize yourself quickly navigating the room, engaging in exciting conversations, and leaving a positive impression. This mental rehearsal primes your subconscious to act out these visualized scenarios, reducing anxiety and boosting confidence.

Adapting to different social contexts requires an acute awareness of the social dynamics at play, which can vary widely from one setting to another. NLP equips you with perceptual positions, a powerful tool for understanding these dynamics from multiple perspectives. By mentally stepping into the shoes of others in the room, you can gain insights into their feelings and motivations and adjust your behavior to better align with the environment. For example, in a formal business networking event, adopting a more formal tone and focusing on professional topics can resonate more effectively with the audience. Conversely, a relaxed demeanor and personal anecdotes might be more appropriate at a casual meet-up. This flexibility in adjusting your communication style and behavior according to the context is critical to social adeptness.

Enhancing essential social skills such as small talk, storytelling, and humor is vital for thriving in social settings. Small talk, often the first step in many social interactions, can be improved through open-ended questions that invite more extended responses. Phrases like "What's your take on...?" or "How did you get involved in...?" can open up the conversation and lead to more meaningful exchanges. On the other hand, storytelling allows you to connect with others emotionally, making your interactions more memorable. NLP techniques can help structure your stories to make them more engaging, using sensory-rich language to paint vivid pictures and evoke emotions. Finally, incorporating humor appropriately can break the ice and make conversations more enjoyable. Observational humor, which involves making light-hearted comments about your immediate surroundings, can be particularly effective as it is relatable and minimizes the risk of offending others.

Building and nurturing a social network is another area where NLP can be incredibly effective. This involves not only making new connections but also deepening existing ones. Regularly contacting your contacts, showing genuine interest in their activities, and offering help or advice where possible can strengthen your social ties. NLP's emphasis on empathy, mirrored in techniques like matching and mirroring, can help you establish a deeper rapport with your contacts, making your interactions more fruitful. By consistently applying these principles, you can create a robust network supporting personal growth and professional advancement.

Incorporating NLP techniques into your social interactions transforms how others perceive you and how you perceive yourself in these settings. Mastering these skills sets the stage for a more confident and proactive approach to social situations, ensuring you survive and thrive in these environments. As you continue to practice and refine these techniques, you will find that what once seemed daunting becomes a wellspring of opportunity, filled with potential for growth, learning, and connection.

5.6 Resolving Conflicts through NLP Frameworks

Conflicts in personal relationships, the workplace, or social interactions often stem from misaligned perceptions, emotions, and communication mishaps. Understanding the psychological and emotional components of these disagreements is crucial. Conflicts typically arise when individuals feel their values are threatened, or their needs are not being met. These situations are often compounded by stress, fear, or historical grievances that can cloud judgment and escalate disputes. Neurolinguistic Programming (NLP) provides a unique approach to addressing these underlying factors, offering strategies that focus on understanding and modifying the perceptions and emotions that fuel conflicts.

One of the core NLP techniques for conflict resolution is reframing. This involves changing the context or perspective on a conflict to alter its meaning and impact on both parties involved. For example, a disagreement in a team setting about project directions can be reframed from a personal power struggle to a shared challenge where every input is aimed at achieving the best outcome for the team. Reframing can transform conflict dynamics by shifting the focus from confrontation to collaboration, fostering a more constructive and less emotionally charged environment. Another powerful NLP tool is the Meta-Model, which consists of questions designed to probe the language used by individuals during a conflict. These questions help clarify vague statements, reveal underlying assumptions, and expose discrepancies in beliefs or understandings. Such clarity can significantly reduce misunderstandings and pave the way for more effective resolutions.

Role-playing is an effective method for practicing these NLP techniques in a safe and controlled setting. By simulating conflict scenarios, individuals can explore various strategies and responses, allowing them to build confidence and skill in handling real-life disputes. For instance, role-playing a workplace conflict scenario where participants alternate between playing the role of a disgruntled employee and a mediating manager can provide valuable insights into the dynamics of conflict and the impact of different resolution strategies. These exercises enhance understanding and improve emotional management, communication skills, and the ability to see conflicts from multiple perspectives.

Preventing future conflicts is equally essential and can be achieved through proactive communication and fostering mutual understanding. NLP encourages the establishment of clear communication channels and norms that promote open expression and timely resolution of issues before they escalate. Techniques such as establishing positive presuppositions—assuming the best intentions in others—can create a more trusting and open atmosphere. Regular feedback sessions and establishing agreed-upon communication models, such as regular team check-ins or family meetings, can help maintain this environment, ensuring that potential conflicts are managed constructively and promptly.

By integrating these NLP frameworks into your conflict resolution repertoire, you become adept at managing and resolving disputes and preventing them from arising. These skills are invaluable in navigating the complexities of interpersonal relationships and professional environments, contributing to healthier, more productive interactions and outcomes.

As we conclude this exploration of enhancing interpersonal relationships through NLP, the techniques and strategies discussed provide a robust foundation for resolving conflicts and building deeper connections and understanding in all areas of your life. By applying these principles, you can transform your approach to relationships, fostering environments of cooperation, respect, and mutual growth. The next chapter will describe advanced NLP techniques that expand on these concepts, offering more sophisticated tools for personal development and professional excellence.

6

ADVANCED NLP TECHNIQUES FOR PERSONAL DEVELOPMENT

P icture yourself not as a mere spectator but as an active participant in your past, capable of reshaping your experiences and their emotional impacts. This is not a plot from a science fiction novel but the unique promise of Timeline Therapy, a Neurolinguistic Programming technique that empowers you to revisit and reconstruct your past. This chapter explores this distinctive approach, guiding you through the processes that can free you from historical and emotional burdens and help you rewrite your life narrative toward positivity and growth.

6.1 Timeline Therapy: Revisiting and Reshaping Your Past

Concept of Timeline Therapy

Timeline Therapy is based on the premise that our memories and the emotions associated with them are arranged along a mental timeline. This therapy involves navigating this timeline to access and modify troubling past events that continue to impact your emotional well-being. Developed within the realm of NLP, this technique is predicated on the understanding that negative emotions and limiting decisions from the past can be released to heal emotional traumas and reshape experiences. Unlike traditional therapies that often focus extensively on the analytical exploration of past events, Timeline Therapy provides a dynamic process to transform your emotional landscape actively, focusing more on how you encode your experiences rather than the factual details.

Process of Revisiting Past Events

Your journey through the timeline begins with identifying an initial sensitizing event, often the first or the most impactful event that triggers a negative emotional response. Whether guided by a trained NLP practitioner or through self-guided techniques, you will revisit this event not to relive the pain but to understand and reframe its impact. This is done from a dissociated perspective, ensuring you view the events as if you were a bystander, thus reducing the emotional charge and providing a clearer view of the incident's broader context. This vantage point allows you to extract valuable lessons while leaving behind the emotional burden. The safety and control you feel during this process are paramount, especially when dealing with deeply traumatic events, ensuring you navigate through these memories with confidence and efficacy.

Reshaping Past Narratives

Armed with new insights, you then alter the past event's narrative. This involves changing the submodalities of the memory—such as dimming the colors, adjusting the sounds, or altering the perceived distance—which helps to decrease its negative emotional impact. You might also introduce new, empowering elements to the memory, such as resources you now possess that you didn't have at the time of the event. For example, you could imagine your present self offering support or advice to your past self. This not only helps in reinterpreting the event but also instills a sense of empowerment and reassurance, boosting your confidence and self-assurance.

Practical Applications and Benefits

The transformative power of Timeline Therapy is extensive and primarily centered around increased emotional freedom and personal empowerment. By releasing the negative emotional hold of past events, you can experience a significant reduction in anxiety, anger, sadness, and fear, leading to a more balanced and positive emotional state. This emotional clearance sets the stage for more personal growth and self-development. Furthermore, Timeline Therapy can enhance your self-awareness and expand your understanding of how past influences shape your current behaviors and decisions. This understanding is critical as it empowers you to make more conscious, aligned choices about responding to current and future events, steering your life trajectory towards desired outcomes.

Interactive Element: Timeline Exploration Exercise

To begin exploring the benefits of Timeline Therapy, engage in this initial exercise. Reflect on an event from your past that still evokes a strong emotional response. Write down a brief description of this event, focusing on how it made you feel rather than the intricate details of what happened. Then, visualize yourself stepping out of your body and observing the event from a distance as if you were watching it on a screen. Notice any changes in your emotional response as you alter the visual and auditory submodalities of the memory. This exercise is foundational in understanding how Timeline Therapy can shift your emotional perspective on past events, leading to healing and growth. Remember, this technique, especially when dealing with deeply traumatic events, is best navigated with the support of a qualified NLP practitioner to ensure safety and efficacy.

This exploration into Timeline Therapy reveals one of the many ways advanced NLP techniques can foster significant personal development. By learning to master and apply these strategies, you unlock the potential to reshape your past and sculpt a future that reflects your true aspirations and potential.

6.2 Advanced Anchoring for Complex Emotional States

Anchoring, a foundational concept within Neurolinguistic Programming, extends beyond simple emotional triggers. It harnesses your sensory experiences to create robust responses you can activate on demand. This technique is particularly effective in complex and layered emotional states where multiple feelings or reactions intertwine. Advanced anchoring involves not merely creating a link between a stimulus and a desired emotional state but layering and integrating multiple anchors to handle more nuanced emotional landscapes. This deep dive into advanced anchoring will elucidate how to craft and utilize these compound anchors, ensuring they are robust enough to withstand various challenges and remain effective.

Creating compound anchors begins with the identification and combination of multiple sensory modalities. Consider a scenario where you must simultaneously evoke a state of calm, focus, and confidence—perhaps for a significant professional presentation. You might start by recalling an experience where you felt exceptionally calm. As you relive this memory, identify a specific sensory trigger—perhaps the feel of cool air on your skin. Next, recall an instance of deep focus, maybe while engaged in a favorite hobby. The sound of a ticking clock in the background could be the anchor. Finally, bring to mind a moment of peak confidence, and let the bright color of the room in your memory be the trigger. By combining these sensory triggers—cool air, the ticking sound, and vivid color— you create a compound anchor that encapsulates all these states, ready to be activated when you step up to deliver your presentation.

Strategies for layering these anchors effectively require careful planning and practice. The process involves gradually building a 'stack' of emotional states that can be triggered sequentially or simultaneously. Start with the most funda- mental emotional state you wish to anchor. Once this anchor is set and reliably triggers the desired emotional response, introduce the next sensory trigger while in the state evoked by the first anchor. This layering can create a cascade of emotional states that are intricately linked and easily accessible. Regularly revisiting and reinforcing these compound anchors is crucial, especially in different contexts and emotional states, to ensure their stability and effectiveness.

Incorporating real-world applications and case studies can illustrate the impact of advanced anchoring. Consider the case of a veteran firefighter who used compound anchoring to manage emergencies' intense stress and emotional turmoil. He could maintain clarity and composure during critical operations by establishing a series of anchors associated with calmness, focus, and resilience, triggered by specific tactile and auditory cues in his gear and environment. Another example involves a public speaker who overcame severe stage fright through a series of layered anchors involving scents, sounds, and tactile sensations that together evoked a state of calm assertiveness, enabling her to deliver speeches with confidence and dynamism.

These examples underscore the versatility and effectiveness of advanced anchoring in managing complex emotional states, particularly in high-pressure or challenging environments. By mastering this technique, you can equip yourself with a powerful tool for emotional regulation that enhances your performance and well-being across various personal and professional settings. As you continue to explore and integrate these advanced anchoring strategies, you will find yourself more adept at navigating the complexities of your emotional landscape, leading to more personal mastery and fulfillment.

6.3 Meta Programs: Understanding Personal Behavioral Patterns

Meta Programs in Neurolinguistic Programming (NLP) are

robust internal processes that influence how you interpret the world and make decisions. These cognitive patterns act like lenses, coloring your perceptions and behaviors consistently. Understanding Meta Programs is akin to unveiling the operating system of your mind—it shows you how you run your mental programs to feel, think, and act in various situations. Each person utilizes a variety of Meta Programs, and these patterns significantly shape their personality, motivation, and actions. For instance, one typical Meta Program distinguishes between individuals who are oriented toward achieving goals (toward) versus those who are motivated to solve problems (away from). This distinction can affect one's approach to work and personal challenges.

The process of identifying your dominant Meta Programs involves keen self-observation and reflection. Consider how you typically respond to daily situations or make decisions. Are you more motivated by potential gains or the need to avoid losses? Do you generally prefer to dive into specifics or think broadly? Responses to such questions can help pinpoint your predominant Meta Programs. For instance, if you meticulously plan every project detail, you might operate under a 'detail-oriented' Meta Program. Conversely, if you prefer to delegate specifics and focus on the big picture, you might be guided by a 'global-thinking' Meta Program. Recognizing these patterns provides critical insights into your inherent predispositions and how they influence your interactions and decisions.

Harnessing the awareness of Meta Programs in personal development involves using this knowledge to tailor your approach to various situations for better outcomes. If you know you are primarily motivated by goal achievement, you can structure your tasks to highlight these outcomes, enhancing your motivation. Conversely, understanding that you have a strong avoidance pattern might lead you to reframe tasks as opportunities to prevent adverse outcomes, thus aligning your natural inclinations with necessary activities. This strategic self-awareness allows you to navigate your personal and professional life more effectively, adapting your approach to better suit your psychological predispositions.

To experiment with and modify your Meta Programs, engage in exercises that challenge your default settings. For example, if you are naturally detail-oriented, practice taking a global view of a project by focusing only on its key objectives and outcomes. Conversely, if you typically focus on the big picture, try breaking a project down into detailed steps and concentrating on each step. This practice enhances flexibility in switching between different cognitive styles and broadens your behavioral repertoire, making you more adaptable and effective in diverse situations. Regularly engaging in such exercises can significantly improve how you manage tasks, relate with others, and achieve your goals.

You better understand your cognitive and behavioral patterns by actively identifying, understanding, and modifying your Meta Programs. This knowledge enhances self-awareness and empowers you to make deliberate changes that improve your interactions and decision-making processes. As you continue to explore and adjust your Meta Programs, you'll likely discover more nuanced aspects of your personality and behavior, each providing new opportunities for personal growth and development.

6.4 Utilizing NLP for Habit Change

Understanding how habits are formed and subsequently encoded in your brain is pivotal for personal and professional growth. From a Neurolinguistic Programming (NLP) perspective, habits are essentially patterns of behavior that are repeated until they become automatic responses. These routines are stored in your brain's neural pathways, becoming your default actions under certain conditions. When a particular stimulus is presented, it triggers a specific neural pathway, leading to the associated behavior. This process is efficient for the brain but can be detrimental when the automatic behavior is undesirable. The good news is that just as these pathways were developed, they can also be altered. Your brain's neuroplasticity allows for rewiring these pathways, creating new, more beneficial habits.

Breaking unwanted habits with NLP involves interrupting these ingrained neurological patterns. The first step is identifying the trigger for the habit you want to change. This could be a specific time of day, emotional state, or sequence of events that usually leads to the unwanted behavior. Once identified, NLP techniques such as pattern interrupts can be employed. These techniques involve introducing a sudden, unexpected action or thought that disrupts the automatic sequence, leading to the undesired behavior. For instance, if you have a habit of mindlessly snacking while watching TV, you might choose to clap your hands loudly each time you reach for a snack. This interruption redirects your brain's attention and weakens the existing neural pathway, making it easier to introduce a healthier response, like reaching for a glass of water instead.

Creating desirable habits using NLP is not just about stopping a behavior but about replacing it with a more constructive one. This is where the concept of patterning comes into play. Patterning involves designing a new sequence of actions that leads to a positive outcome and repeating this pattern until it becomes the new automatic response. The use of positive reinforcement enhances this process. Each time a new behavior is performed, it should be followed by a rewarding experience, which could be internal praise, a small treat, or another form of positive feedback. This reinforcement makes the new behavior more appealing to the brain, increasing the likelihood of the new habit becoming entrenched. For example, if your goal is to improve your physical fitness, you might start a new habit of morning exercises. Following each workout, you could reward yourself with a few moments of relaxation or a healthy smoothie, linking the exercise with a pleasurable reward.

Sustaining change over time requires continuous practice and self-reflection. This is crucial because the brain needs consistent reinforcement to maintain the new neural pathways you've worked hard to establish. Regular reflection on your progress helps you stay committed to your new habits and allows you to adjust your strategies as needed. Keeping a habit journal can be an effective way to track your behaviors, triggers, and the effectiveness of your NLP techniques. In this journal, record each instance of successfully performing the new habit and note how you felt afterward. Also, document the moments you revert to old behaviors and explore what triggered the relapse. This ongoing monitoring and reflection notch incremental changes that, over time, result in a substantial transformation.

Through these detailed discussions on breaking old habits and creating new ones, it becomes evident that NLP offers a robust framework for effecting lasting change. By understanding the mechanics of habit formation and applying targeted NLP techniques, you can reprogram your behaviors to better align with your goals and values. As you continue to practice these strategies, you transform your habits and empower yourself to take proactive control over your actions and reactions, paving the way for a more disciplined and fulfilling life.

6.5 The Milton Model: Hypnotic Language Patterns

The Milton Model, named after the psychiatrist Milton H. Erickson, is a cornerstone of Neurolinguistic Programming that focuses on the strategic use of language to influence and communicate on a subconscious level. Erickson was renowned for his innovative approach to psychotherapy, where he utilized ambiguous and symbolic language to facilitate change without resistance from the patient. This model is particularly noted for its ability to bypass the analytical mind and speak directly to the subconscious, allowing for subtle yet therapeutic transformations. The essence of the Milton Model lies in its foundational premise that the subconscious mind can process vague statements and metaphors more effectively than it can direct commands, often met with internal opposition (Dilts 1999).

The techniques of the Milton Model are diverse. Still, they share a common goal: to create a more receptive communication channel that encourages the listener to fill in the gaps with their own experiences and insights, thereby fostering a deeper personal connection to the message. One of the fundamental techniques is using vague language, which intentionally needs more specificity. This might sound counterintuitive in contexts where clarity is valued. Still, in the therapeutic setting, such ambiguity encourages the client to draw upon their meanings and interpretations, engaging more deeply with the process. Another technique uses embedded commands and instructions within a more significant sentence, camouflaged by the linguistic structure. For example, in the sentence, "Many find it comforting to learn new things," the embedded command "learn new things" is subtly highlighted by the tonal emphasis, encouraging the listener to engage in learning without directly telling them to do so.

In everyday communication, the Milton Model proves to be an invaluable tool for anyone looking to enhance their persuasive and influential capabilities. Whether you are a leader trying to inspire your team, a therapist aiding clients, or someone looking to improve interpersonal communications, these techniques can elevate the effectiveness of your interactions. By framing suggestions in a way that resonates on a subconscious level, you can encourage others toward positive change subtly and ethically. For instance, a manager might use metaphors to depict a vision of a project's potential success, motivating the team through imagery and emotion rather than direct instruction, which might meet resistance.

To master hypnotic language patterns, consider engaging in exercises to enhance linguistic flexibility and subtlety. Start by practicing the art of crafting metaphors that relate to everyday experiences but allow for individual interpretation. For example, compare a business challenge to navigating a ship through a storm. This metaphor not only invokes the imagery of teamwork and adventure but also allows individuals to connect their personal feelings about overcoming difficulties. Another exercise is to transform direct instructions into embedded commands within casual conversation. Practice embedding these commands by subtly changing your tone to emphasize the critical parts of the sentence. Over time, these practices will enhance your ability to communicate more effectively, influencing others respectfully.

These techniques and exercises enrich your communication skills and deepen your understanding of how language shapes thought and behavior. As you continue to explore and apply the Milton Model, you'll likely discover a newfound appreciation for the power of words and their impact on the mind, opening up new avenues for personal and professional growth.

6.6 Modeling Excellence: Learning from the Best

Modeling in the context of Neurolinguistic Programming (NLP) is a powerful approach that involves observing and replicating exemplary performers' behaviors, thought processes, and success strategies in any field. This technique is rooted in the belief that if one person can achieve a particular level of success, then it is possible to decode the underlying patterns and strategies that contributed to their success, and by learning and applying these, others can achieve similar results. The essence of modeling in NLP is not about mere imitation but understanding the deep structures of excellence in others so that you can adapt these to enhance your skills and abilities.

The process of effective modeling involves several critical steps. Initially, it requires identifying a role model whose skills or achievements align with the outcomes you desire. This could be a leader in your industry, a sports professional, or even a public speaker whose abilities you admire. The next step is to analyze the behavior patterns of this individual. Pay attention to what they do and how they do it—including their body language, mental focus during tasks, and the beliefs that drive their actions. This analysis should be thorough and nuanced, capturing their performance's overt and subtle elements.

Once you have gathered this information, adapting these observed behaviors and mental strategies to your context is challenging. This means something other than copying them exactly but translating their strategies into actions applicable to your personal or professional life. For instance, if you are modeling a skilled communicator, you might adopt their way of engaging with an audience, their use of storytelling, or their methods of handling questions and objections and then integrate these skills into your presentations or meetings.

Real-life examples of successful modeling abound in various fields. Consider a young entrepreneur who dramatically improved her business strategies by modeling a successful business leader. She observed that her role model used a specific method for strategic planning and stakeholder engagement. By adapting these strategies to her business, she expanded her company's market reach and profitability. Another example is a therapist who enhanced his therapeutic techniques by modeling a renowned psychologist. He noticed that the psychologist used unique questioning techniques to explore clients' issues deeply. By incorporating these questioning styles into his practice, he significantly improved his ability to help clients achieve breakthroughs in therapy.

Guidelines for Ethical Modeling

While modeling is a powerful tool for learning and development, it comes with the responsibility to uphold ethical standards. Ethical modeling ensures that your adoption of another's strategies or behaviors is transparent and does not infringe on intellectual property or personal rights. It is also essential to maintain authenticity while adopting observed behaviors. This means adapting what you learn to fit your values and unique personality rather than attempting to become a carbon copy of someone else. Moreover, ethical modeling respects the original context in which these behaviors were effective, considering cultural and situational differences that might influence their applicability in new settings.

Modeling in NLP provides a pragmatic route to personal development and success based on the principle that skills and excellence can be learned and replicated. By carefully selecting role models, analyzing their success patterns, and ethically adapting these to your own life, you can accelerate your learning process and significantly advance your capabilities. This approach enhances your skill set and empowers you to contribute more effectively to your profession or community, driving success in a way that is inspired and grounded in proven strategies.

6.7 Summary of recent research

Recent publications on neurolinguistic programming (NLP) cover a range of applications and findings:

1 **The effect of neurolinguistic programming on academic achievement, emotional intelligence, and critical thinking of EFL learners:** This study found that NLP techniques can significantly improve academic performance, emotional intelligence,

and critical thinking skills among English as a Foreign Language (EFL) learners (Zhang, Davarpanah, & Izadpanah, 2023).

2 Neuro-linguistic programming as an instructional strategy to enhance foreign language teaching: This paper highlights the effectiveness of using NLP as a teaching strategy to improve foreign language learning. It suggests NLP can enhance language acquisition and teaching methodologies (Purnama et al., 2023).

3 Development of neurolinguistic programming module for golf athletes: A needs analysis: The research indicates that an NLP module can be a valuable addition to psychological training programs for athletes, specifically improving their performance and mental toughness in golf (Muniandy, Rasyid & Abdul Razak, 2023).

4 The concept of neuro-linguistic programming in improving the receptive skills in English: This article explores the application of NLP in enhancing English learners' receptive skills (listening and reading), demonstrating positive impacts on language proficiency (Rogers, 2023).

5 Neuro-linguistic programming and learning theory: A response: This response paper examines the theoretical foundations of NLP and its implications for learning theory. It discusses the potential benefits and critiques of integrating NLP into educational practices (Tosey & Mathison, 2023).

6 Neurolinguistic programming: Old wine in new glass: This article examines the historical and contemporary perspectives on neurolinguistic programming (NLP). It explores the methodologies and impact of NLP over the years, offering a critical view of its applications and effectiveness (Bhugra & Tasman, 2024).

7 Scientific status of neuro-linguistic programming and discoursologic analysis of linguistic aspect: The article highlights the ongoing scientific debate regarding the legitimacy and effectiveness of NLP. It discusses various linguistic aspects and critiques the current methodologies used in NLP research (Velichko, Ivanov, & Smirnov, 2023).

8 Neuro Linguistic Programming: An Effective Tool for Teaching: This study investigates how NLP can be utilized as a tool in the teaching domain. It examines how NLP can enhance learning and improve educational outcomes (Singh & Kaur, 2023).

9 Pseudoscience: A Review of Neuro-Linguistic Programming (NLP): This review paper scrutinizes NLP as a pseudoscience. It provides a comprehensive literature review, highlighting the controversies and the lack of empirical support for many NLP claims (Brandeis, 2024).

10   Evidence-based neurolinguistic psychotherapy: A meta-analysis: This meta-analysis by Zaharia, Reiner, and Schutz examines the effectiveness of neuro-linguistic psychotherapy (NLPt) using evidence-based research. The study aggregates data from multiple studies to evaluate the therapeutic outcomes of NLPt. The findings suggest that NLPt is an effective intervention for various psychological conditions, demonstrating significant improvements in mental health outcomes compared to control groups. The authors conclude that NLPt has a solid evidence base, supporting its use as a viable therapeutic approach. However, they also call for further research to strengthen the evidence and address any methodological limitations in the existing studies (Zaharia & Schutz, 2015).

As we conclude this exploration of advanced NLP techniques, we connect these productive strategies to the broader journey of personal and professional excellence. Each method, from Timeline Therapy to Modeling Excellence, offers unique tools for changing behaviors and fostering deep-seated growth and understanding of the self. As you move forward, these techniques provide a foundation for continuous learning and improvement, equipping you to face future challenges with confidence and skill. Stay tuned for the upcoming chapter, where we dive deeper into practical applications of NLP in everyday scenarios, ensuring that you are well-prepared to apply these powerful strategies in real-world contexts.

7

NLP APPLICATIONS IN DAILY LIFE

As dawn breaks and a new day begins, the power to set a robust and upbeat tone for the hours ahead is in your hands. This isn't just about reacting to life as it happens; it's about proactively shaping your day from the very start with intention and insight, using the empowering principles of Neurolinguistic Programming (NLP). This chapter shows how integrating NLP into your morning routine can significantly boost your mental and physical readiness, paving the way for a day marked by accomplishment and positivity. It's about taking control of your day right from the start, feeling empowered and proactive.

7.1 Morning NLP Routines for a Successful Day
Establishing a Morning Mindset

The quiet of the morning presents a unique opportunity to influence your mindset before the day's demands take hold. Engaging with NLP techniques such as affirmations and visualizations can significantly impact your psychological state, fostering a successful mindset. Affirmations in NLP are not mere positive statements but strategic, crafted declarations that reprogram your subconscious to align with your goals and values. By starting your day reciting tailored affirmations, you affirm your ability to handle whatever comes your way with competence and confidence.

Visualization, another potent NLP technique, involves vividly imagining the successful outcomes of your day's tasks. This process not only primes your mind to pursue these outcomes but also conditions your emotional responses to align with a state of achievement and satisfaction. For instance, visualize a challenging meeting: see yourself speaking confidently, feel the room's positive response, and imagine the sense of accomplishment that follows a successful interaction. This mental rehearsal sets a robust, positive trajectory for the actual event.

Routine NLP Exercises

Regular exercises that prime your neuro-linguistic pathways are essential to fully integrating NLP into your morning routine. Mental rehearsals, as mentioned, are a cornerstone of this practice. Each morning, dedicate a few moments to mentally walk through critical engagements of the day, paying close attention to your desired behaviors and outcomes. Additionally, setting clear, intentional statements about your daily goals can align your subconscious with your conscious actions. This may be like setting an intention to remain open and adaptive, preparing you to handle unexpected developments gracefully and flexibly.

Another effective morning exercise involves practicing the 'Circle of Excellence,' an NLP technique where you visualize a circle on the ground filled with qualities you need for the day, such as calmness, clarity, or confidence. Step into this circle and allow yourself to fully experience these qualities, affirming their presence in your day. This boosts your mood and anchors these states, making them more accessible throughout the day. To practice this, find a quiet space where you can stand comfortably. Visualize a circle on the ground in front of you, filled with the qualities you need for the day. Step into this circle, feeling the qualities fill you up. Spend a few moments fully experiencing these qualities, then step out of the circle, carrying these feelings with you into your day.

Integrating NLP with Physical Activities

Combining NLP techniques with morning physical activities can amplify the benefits of both. For instance, if you practice yoga or a morning walk, use this time to integrate affirmations or visualization. As you move your body, recite affirmations reinforcing your physical and mental health, or visualize your day unfolding positively with each step or pose. This integration enhances the mind-body connection, boosting energy levels and mental clarity.

Examples of Successful Morning Routines

Consider the routine of a renowned CEO who attributes her clarity and leadership success to her NLP-enhanced morning routine. She begins her day with a 20-minute meditation incorporating visualizations of her crucial leadership tasks. Following this, she recites affirmations about her capabilities and goals during her morning jog. This routine prepares her mentally and physically and aligns her subconscious with her conscious goals, significantly impacting her effectiveness and resilience.

Similarly, a tech entrepreneur starts his day with a combination of the 'Circle of Excellence' exercise followed by a brisk walk during which he mentally rehearses upcoming pitches and meetings, using visualization to anticipate challenges and responses. This preparation has been crucial in his successful negotiations and business growth, demonstrating the impact of a well-constructed morning routine.

Incorporating these NLP strategies into your morning routine can transform ordinary mornings into powerful launches into successful days. By consciously engaging your mind and body in positive, goal-oriented activities right from the start, you set a precedent for the rest of your day, enhancing your productivity, emotional well-being, and overall life satisfaction. As you adopt and adapt these practices, you'll find that each morning brings a renewed sense of purpose and a more straightforward path to achieving your goals, making every day a step towards tremendous success and fulfillment.

7.2 Using NLP to Overcome Daily Stressors

In the ebb and flow of daily life, stress is as inevitable as the clock's ticking. Yet, not all stress must lead to discomfort or disruption. Through Neurolinguistic Programming (NLP), you can transform your approach to stress, turning potential setbacks into opportunities for growth and resilience. The first step in this process involves the identification of stress triggers. NLP equips you with observational and reflective techniques that help pinpoint these triggers accurately. By maintaining a heightened awareness of your emotional responses throughout the day, you can begin to notice patterns. For instance, does your stress spike during certain types of meetings at work or perhaps when handling specific tasks at home? Recognizing these patterns prepares you mentally and emotionally to face them more effectively.

Once you have identified your stress triggers, employing quick and effective NLP techniques can help manage stress on the go. The 'Circle of Excellence' is an excellent tool for this purpose. Whenever you anticipate a stressful situation, mentally step into this circle. Imagine absorbing these qualities, allowing them to enhance your emotional and mental state, preparing you to handle the problem with a heightened sense of control and competence. Similarly, anchoring, which involves associating a physical gesture with relaxation or peace, can be a quick stress-relief tool. For example, gently pressing your thumb and forefinger while recalling a peaceful memory can help invoke calmness whenever you feel overwhelmed.

For long-term stress management, NLP offers strategies to

change the perception of stressors and improve emotional resilience. This approach is rooted in the understanding that stress is not just about external triggers but also our internal responses to these triggers. By altering your perception, you can reduce the impact of stress. Techniques such as reframing enable you to view stressful situations from different perspectives, seeing them as challenges or opportunities for learning rather than threats. This subtle shift in viewpoint can significantly decrease the emotional weight of the stressor, making it more manageable. Building emotional resilience is another crucial aspect, which involves strengthening your emotional response to adversity. Regular practice of NLP techniques like positive affirmations and visualization can reinforce your mental fortitude, enabling you to face stress with a more robust and resilient mindset.

In real-life applications, these NLP strategies prove to be invaluable tools. Consider a professional facing imminent deadlines at work. By identifying the specific aspects of the situation that trigger stress—such as the fear of not meeting expectations—they can apply the 'Circle of Excellence' to instill focus and efficiency. During intense pressure, using an anchor like a reassuring hand gesture while recalling a successful project can provide a quick return to a state of calm and control. Another scenario might involve a social setting where the pressure to interact can induce anxiety. Here, reframing the situation as an opportunity to learn about others and share interesting personal insights rather than as a test of social skills can alleviate stress and enhance the quality of interaction.

These examples underscore the practicality and effectiveness of NLP in managing daily stress. Integrating these techniques into your routine transforms your day-to-day experiences, changing how you perceive and react to stress. This improves your immediate responses and contributes to a long-term enhancement of your mental health and well-being.

As you continue to practice and refine these strategies, you'll find that you are surviving daily challenges and thriving amidst them, equipped with the tools to turn stress into a catalyst for personal growth and success.

7.3 Enhancing Personal Productivity with NLP

In the fast-paced rhythm of today's world, personal productivity is not just a metric of output but a critical component of professional success and personal satisfaction. Neurolinguistic Programming (NLP) offers robust techniques that can significantly influence your ability to set, pursue, and achieve productivity goals. You can define clear and attainable goals using well-formed outcomes—a fundamental NLP tool. This technique involves specifying your goal in sensory-based language, describing what you will see, hear, and feel when you achieve the goal. This clarity transforms abstract aspirations into concrete targets, making them more tangible and achievable.

Visualization complements this by engaging the mind in a dynamic rehearsal of success scenarios. Regular visualization fosters a mental and emotional alignment with your goals, enhancing motivation and focus. For instance, if your goal is to improve your professional skills, visualize yourself attending training sessions, engaging with the material, and applying the knowledge in your work setting. Feel the satisfaction of mastering new skills and the opportunities that unfold. This vivid mental rehearsal primes your subconscious to recognize and seize opportunities for achievement, accelerating your progress toward your goals.

Procrastination often acts as a significant barrier to productivity. NLP addresses this challenge by uncovering the subconscious thought patterns that lead to procrastination. Techniques such as linguistic patterns can alter these ingrained habits. For example, changing your internal dialogue from "I have to complete this task" to "I choose to complete this task because it brings me closer to my goals" can shift your perception of the task from being an imposition to a step towards your success.

Additionally, pattern interruptions—sudden, unexpected changes in thought or behavior—can break the cycle of procrastination. A simple pattern interrupt could be physically moving to a different workspace or altering your work sequence to disrupt the procrastination pattern and stimulate engagement with your tasks.

Optimizing daily schedules using NLP involves strategic planning that aligns with your peak mental and emotional states. Recognize the times of day when you are most energetic and alert, and schedule your most challenging tasks for these periods. Use anchoring techniques to create triggers that signal the start of intensive work periods. For example, a specific playlist could be your anchor for deep work sessions, signaling to your brain that it is time to focus intensely. This conditioning helps transition your mind into a state of productivity more quickly and sustainably.

The impact of these techniques is not merely theoretical but is evidenced in numerous success stories. Consider the case of a software developer plagued by chronic procrastination and unmet deadlines. He could redefine his work goals as exciting challenges rather than mundane obligations by applying NLP techniques, precisely well-formed outcomes, and visualization. He visualized the successful completion of his projects and the subsequent career advancement, which significantly boosted his intrinsic motivation. He used pattern interruptions to combat procrastination, such as changing his work environment and scheduling short, focused work sessions, dramatically improving his productivity.

Another compelling case involves a marketing professional struggling to manage her time effectively, leading to stress and burnout. She implemented NLP strategies to optimize her daily schedule, identifying her peak productivity times and tailoring her work commitments to these periods. She also used anchoring techniques, with specific scents diffused in her workspace to signal times for creative work and different scents for administrative tasks. This sensory differentiation helped her transition more seamlessly between various types of work, enhancing her overall efficiency and job satisfaction.

These examples underscore NLP's practical applications and benefits in enhancing personal productivity. By integrating these strategies into your daily routine, you can transform your approach to work and individual projects, turning everyday tasks into opportunities for success and fulfillment. As you continue to explore and apply these techniques, you will likely discover an improvement in your ability to achieve your goals, making each day more productive and rewarding.

7.4 NLP Techniques for Decision Making

Decision-making is an art refined by the clarity and precision of your thoughts. Neurolinguistic Programming (NLP) enhances these aspects, improving decision-making skills by focusing on how we process information and anticipate outcomes. The ability to foresee consequences is not just about predicting the future; it's about understanding the implications of your choices and recognizing potential obstacles and opportunities. NLP techniques, such as visualizing potential outcomes, can significantly enhance this ability. You engage your conscious and subconscious mind in a dynamic evaluation process by vividly imagining the results of different decisions. This mental simulation clarifies what might happen and primes your mind to deal with potential scenarios, making you better prepared to make decisions that align with your goals and values.

Balancing emotional and rational thoughts in decision-making is crucial. Emotions can provide signals about our values and fears and cloud our judgment. NLP offers tools to manage and balance these emotional influences. Techniques such as the emotional reframing method allow you to acknowledge your emotions and then consciously view the decision rationally. This might involve asking yourself specific questions to challenge emotional responses, such as, "What are the facts of this situation?" or "What would I advise a friend to do in this instance?" By systematically addressing your decisions' emotional and rational aspects, you ensure that your choices are emotionally satisfying and logically sound.

Introducing specific NLP models can further refine your decision-making process. One such model is the TOTE model (Test-Operate-Test-Exit), which provides a clear decision-making framework. The process starts with a 'Test' phase, where you define what success looks like. In the 'Operate' phase, you take action to achieve this success. You then 'Test' again to see if your criteria for success have been met. If they have, you 'Exit' the process; if not, modify your approach and repeat the cycle. This model encourages a systematic approach to decision-making, ensuring thorough consideration and flexibility to adapt as needed. Another strategy involves using decision-making matrices that help weigh different factors and potential outcomes, providing a structured way to evaluate options and make more informed choices.

Practical Decision-Making Exercises

To effectively integrate these NLP techniques into your daily decision-making, consider engaging in specific exercises designed to enhance your skills. One powerful exercise is the 'Best/Worst Analysis,' where you visualize a decision's best and worst possible outcomes. Start by identifying a decision you need to make. Imagine the best possible outcome, focusing on the details and the steps you took to achieve this scenario. Then, do the same for the worst possible outcome. This exercise helps evaluate the risks and benefits of the decision and prepares you mentally to handle any potential consequences, reducing anxiety and uncertainty.

Another valuable exercise involves role-playing different decision-making scenarios. This can be particularly effective in a group setting where multiple perspectives can be explored. Each participant takes on a different role or perspective in decision-making, such as a stakeholder, critic, or advocate. By arguing from these perspectives, you gain a broader understanding of the implications of your decisions, which can lead to more robust and sustainable outcomes.

Regular practice of these exercises can transform your decision-making process, making it more deliberate, informed, and balanced. Whether you are deciding on career moves, personal investments, or daily operational choices, these NLP strategies provide a solid foundation for making rational decisions aligned with your more personal and professional aspirations. As you continue to apply and refine these techniques, you will notice a significant enhancement in your confidence and competence in making decisions, empowering you to take charge of your life with clarity and purpose.

7.5 Using NLP for Physical Health and Well-being

The intimate connection between the mind and body is a cornerstone of Neurolinguistic Programming (NLP), advocating that our thoughts, emotions, and beliefs impact our physical health. This interplay suggests that modifying our mental patterns can directly influence bodily functions and processes, enhancing overall health and well-being. For instance, how we mentally process stress can affect our immune system, hormonal balance, and cardiovascular health. Understanding this connection allows you to harness NLP techniques not just for mental or emotional improvements but for physical health gains as well.

One of the most potent applications of NLP in physical health is through techniques designed for pain management. Pain, while often a physiological response to stimuli, is also significantly influenced by the mind. How we perceive pain, react to it, and expect it can alter our experience. NLP offers tools such as reframing, which changes pain perception from overwhelmingly negative to a signal that can be managed or interpreted differently. For example, instead of viewing pain as a debilitating factor, you can reframe it as a guide that helps you understand your body better. This shift in perception can reduce the emotional impact of pain, often leading to a decrease in the pain's intensity.

Dissociation is another powerful NLP technique for managing pain. This involves mentally stepping outside oneself to observe the painful experience as if it were happening to someone else. This psychological distance can significantly reduce the immediacy and intensity of pain, making it more manageable. By practicing dissociation, you can navigate painful episodes with a level of detachment that helps manage the discomfort more effectively.

Promoting healthier lifestyle choices is another critical area where NLP proves invaluable. Subconscious patterns and emotional responses govern our eating habits and lifestyle decisions. NLP techniques can help modify these patterns, leading to better choices. For instance, if you eat in response to stress, using NLP to address and reprogram this response can lead to healthier eating patterns. Techniques such as anchoring can create new responses to stress, such as taking a walk or practicing deep-breathing exercises instead of reaching for comfort food.

Moreover, regular physical activity, often a challenge for many due to lack of motivation or negative associations with exercise, can also be enhanced through NLP. Changing the submodalities of how one views exercise—from a chore to a rewarding, enjoyable activity—can significantly alter one's willingness to engage in physical activity. Visualization can play a crucial role here; imagine yourself enjoying a workout and feeling great afterward, which can help transform your attitude towards maintaining an active lifestyle.

The efficacy of these strategies is not merely theoretical but is supported by numerous success stories. Consider the case of a middle-aged woman who has chronic arthritis. Traditional pain management strategies had limited effectiveness. However, by employing NLP techniques of reframing and dissociation, she managed to gain considerable control over her pain perception, which improved her mobility and overall quality of life. Another example is a young professional who struggled with obesity due to unhealthy eating patterns. Through NLP, he was able to identify and modify the subconscious cues that led to his overeating. By creating new, healthier responses to these cues, he lost significant weight and, more importantly, adopted a more nutritious lifestyle long-term.

These stories highlight the power of NLP in enhancing physical health and well-being. By understanding and applying the principles of the mind-body connection and incorporating NLP techniques into your daily routine, you can achieve excellent mental and emotional health and improve your physical well-being. As you continue to explore these techniques, you'll likely discover a holistic improvement in your quality of life, driven by a deeper alignment between your mind and body.

7.6 NLP for Parenting: Techniques for Raising Confident Children

Parenting significantly shapes a child's development. Neurolinguistic Programming (NLP) offers a rich toolbox for enhancing this journey, providing strategies that strengthen the parent-child relationship and foster the growth of confident, resilient children. Understanding and applying NLP techniques can transform your parenting approach, leading to more harmonious interactions and positively impacting your child's development.

Building Rapport with Children

One of the fundamental aspects of effective parenting is building and maintaining a strong rapport with your children. Rapport in this context goes beyond mere affection—it involves a deep understanding and connection that fosters open communication and mutual respect. NLP teaches that rapport with children can be significantly enhanced by adapting to their representational systems—the preferred ways they perceive and process information. For instance, if a child is primarily visual, they might respond better to demonstrations and visual aids rather than verbal instructions. On the other hand, an auditory-dominant child might respond best to discussions and verbal storytelling. By identifying and adapting to these systems, you can communicate more effectively, making your interactions more engaging and understandable for the child. Techniques such as mirroring your child's language patterns, tone, and body language can further deepen this connection, making the child feel seen and understood, thereby fostering a safe and supportive environment conducive to learning and growth.

Enhancing Children's Self-Esteem

NLP also offers powerful strategies for boosting children's self-esteem, which is crucial for their overall emotional and psychological development. Positive reinforcement is an essential technique here—recognizing and praising your child's efforts and achievements, no matter how small. This acknowledgment makes them feel valued and reinforces their desire to engage and persist in activities. Additionally, NLP modeling techniques can be used to teach children by example. By modeling behaviors that reflect confidence and positivity, you provide a live blueprint for the child to emulate. This might involve demonstrating problem-solving in real-time or handling emotional challenges with resilience. Children learn a great deal by observing adults, so consistently displaying qualities you wish to instill in them can be incredibly impactful.

Teaching Resilience and Problem-Solving

Equipping children with resilience and practical problem-solving skills is essential for navigating the complexities of growing up. NLP strategies can be beneficial in this area. Teaching children how to reframe challenges as opportunities for learning is a valuable skill. For example, if a child is upset about a poor performance on a school test, you can guide them to see it as a chance to identify areas for improvement and learn new study techniques. This alleviates the emotional burden and empowers the child to take proactive steps toward improvement. Moreover, NLP techniques such as the 'Disney Strategy,' which involves dreaming up solutions without constraints, can encourage creative problem-solving and innovative thinking in children. By fostering an environment where creative solutions are valued and emotional resilience is nurtured, you prepare your child to face life's challenges with confidence and agility.

Case Studies of NLP in Parenting

The practical applications of NLP in parenting are vast and varied. Consider the case of a parent who used NLP techniques to help their child overcome severe anxiety about school. By teaching the child simple anchoring methods, where the child could trigger feelings of calm and safety through a specific gesture, the child could manage their anxiety effectively, leading to improved school attendance and participation. Another example involves a parent who used reframing and positive reinforcement to help their child deal with bullying. By helping the child reframe the bullies' actions as a reflection of the bullies' insecurities and emphasizing the child's strengths and values, the parent could significantly boost the child's self-esteem and resilience.

These examples illustrate the potential of NLP in parenting.

By incorporating these techniques into your parenting style, you enhance your interactions with your children and equip them with the skills and mindsets necessary for personal success and emotional well-being. As you explore and apply these strategies, you will likely find that NLP improves your effectiveness as a parent and enriches your family life, creating a nurturing environment where each member thrives.

Neurolinguistic Programming can be integrated into daily parenting practices, highlighting its effectiveness in building rapport, enhancing self-esteem, and teaching resilience and problem-solving. As we transition from these foundational aspects of personal development, the next chapter will focus on broader applications of NLP in community and organizational settings, exploring how these powerful techniques can be scaled to influence groups and cultures, further extending the benefits of NLP beyond the personal to the communal.

8

BEYOND TECHNIQUES: BUILDING SUSTAINABLE NLP PRACTICES

Imagine if every reflection in the mirror, every feedback session, and every self-evaluation could be transformed into stepping stones towards undeniable success and self-improvement. In Neurolinguistic Programming (NLP), self-assessment is not just routine—it's a pivotal strategy for personal evolution. This chapter dives into the tools and methods you can employ to critically assess your growth in NLP, ensuring that each step is grounded in self-awareness and directed towards continuous improvement. This process not only guides you but empowers you to take control of your personal and professional growth, leading you towards your desired outcomes.

8.1 Evaluating Your NLP Growth: Self-Assessment Techniques

Self-assessment is a cornerstone of NLP, offering a unique perspective on your growth. It's not just about where you are but where you're headed. Regularly evaluating your progress is like having a mirror that reflects your evolving skills, highlights areas needing attention, and reinforces effective techniques. This reflective practice is fundamental in transitioning from novice to adept, fostering a disciplined, informed approach to personal development.

Developing practical self-assessment tools is your first step toward meaningful evaluations. One powerful tool is the NLP Progress Journal. This personalized journal should detail your experiences with different NLP techniques, the contexts in which you apply them, and the outcomes. It's important to include not just the techniques used, but also your reflections on their effectiveness, any challenges you faced, and your plans for improvement. Regular entries allow you to track patterns and improvements, providing a written record of your journey and growth. To augment the journal, consider implementing structured reflection sessions where you review your weekly or monthly entries to analyze trends and plan future focus areas.

Feedback loops are a vital part of refining your NLP practice. They involve continuously receiving and integrating feedback into your NLP strategies. Start by identifying trusted mentors, peers, or coaches who understand your NLP goals. Arrange regular feedback sessions with them to discuss your progress and receive constructive criticism. Integrating their insights helps you adjust your approach, ensuring your practice remains responsive to your evolving needs and challenges. Moreover, teaching others about NLP can also form a part of your feedback loop. Teaching can reveal gaps in your understanding and encourage you to solidify your knowledge, fostering a sense of community and support in your NLP journey.

To illustrate the power of effective self-assessment, consider these three case examples:

1. **John, a Sales Manager:** John used his NLP skills primarily to improve his persuasive communication. He maintained a detailed journal where he noted each sales pitch and documented the techniques

used and the outcomes achieved. Over time, his journal entries revealed that storytelling and tailored body language significantly increased client engagement. This insight allowed John to refine his approach, focusing more on these practical strategies, resulting in a 20% increase in sales conversion rates.

2. **Linda, a Therapist:** In her practice, Linda applied NLP techniques to help clients overcome anxiety. She conducted monthly reviews of her session notes, identifying which methods were most effective. Linda realized that anchoring techniques, a method in NLP that associates a particular state of mind or emotion with a specific gesture, touch, or sound, yielded high success rates, prompting her to integrate these into her therapy sessions consistently. The feedback from clients provided through follow-up sessions helped her tweak her application of these techniques, enhancing her effectiveness as a therapist.

3. **Alex, a Public Speaker:** Alex used video recordings of his speeches to self-assess. By watching his performances, he noted his use of pauses and vocal modulation and their impact on audience engagement. Feedback from audience surveys after each presentation provided additional insights, which Alex used to adjust his delivery, making his speeches more dynamic and engaging.

These cases underscore how different self-assessment forms can significantly improve NLP practice. Whether through personal journals, feedback from others, or self-observation, these strategies provide a foundation for continuous growth and mastery of NLP. As you move forward, integrating these self-assessment techniques will enhance your NLP skills and empower you to take charge of your personal and professional development, ensuring that you remain on a path of perpetual growth and success.

8.2 Continuing Education in NLP: Resources and Strategies

Neurolinguistic Programming is a dynamic field, constantly evolving with new theories, techniques, and applications. As an NLP practitioner, embracing lifelong learning is not just beneficial—it's essential. Staying updated with the latest advancements in NLP ensures you are equipped with the most effective tools and strategies, enabling you to support those relying on your expertise. Moreover, continuous education in NLP can significantly broaden your understanding of human behavior, enhance your skillset, and open up new professional opportunities, enriching your personal and professional life. The necessity and excitement of staying updated in your field can be a driving force in your NLP journey.

Various resources cater to different learning styles and schedules. Books, for instance, remain a fundamental resource. They provide in-depth knowledge and insights into specific areas of NLP. Titles such as "Frogs into Princes" by Richard Bandler and John Grinder (1979) or "Introducing NLP" by Joseph O'Connor and John Seymour (1990) offer foundational knowledge and practical insights crucial for beginners and advanced practitioners. Additionally, attending workshops and conferences provides a dynamic learning environment where you can gain hands-on experience with new techniques. These events provide the latest NLP knowledge and offer the opportunity to network with other NLP professionals, which can lead to collaborations and growth opportunities.

Online courses and webinars have become increasingly popular, especially for those seeking flexible learning arrangements. Platforms like Udemy, Coursera, and others offer a range of NLP courses that cover various topics from beginner to advanced levels. These platforms often provide interactive components such as forums and live sessions, allowing for a more engaged learning experience. Furthermore, enrolling in certified NLP training programs can benefit those who prefer a more structured learning path. These programs often lead to certification, enhancing your credibility and professional standing. This adaptability and flexibility make NLP education accessible and able to fit into your life, no matter how busy or varied your schedule may be.

Creating a personal learning plan is a strategic approach to your NLP education. Start by defining clear learning objectives based on your current expertise level and future career goals. Are you looking to strengthen your foundational skills, or are you interested in specializing in areas such as NLP for leadership, coaching, or therapy? Once your goals are set, select resources that best fit your learning style and schedule. Allocate regular time in your calendar for learning activities, whether reading, taking online courses, or attending seminars. It's also beneficial to include practical application in your plan. Regularly practicing new techniques in real-world scenarios helps to consolidate your learning and improve your proficiency.

The benefits of ongoing education in NLP are manifold. Engaging continually with new educational resources keeps you at the forefront of the field and invigorates your practice with fresh ideas and perspectives. It enhances your ability to help others effectively, making your work more fulfilling and impactful. Expanding your knowledge and skills opens new career advancement and professional development avenues. Whether you specialize in a niche area of NLP or broaden your range of practice, continuous education supports your growth and adaptability in an ever-changing field.

Incorporating these strategies into your professional life

will ensure that your NLP practice remains vibrant and compelling, allowing you to meet the diverse needs of those you work with and maintain a fulfilling career in the dynamic field of Neurolinguistic Programming.

8.3 Building an NLP Support Community

Pursuing mastery in Neurolinguistic Programming (NLP) is not a solitary endeavor. The true essence of NLP's power becomes most apparent and accessible when shared within a community. Engaging with a network of NLP practitioners enriches your learning experience, provides emotional and professional support, and opens up myriad opportunities for collaboration and innovation. In such communities, both novices and seasoned professionals exchange insights, challenge each other's understanding, and support personal and collective growth, which are pivotal in navigating the ever-evolving landscape of NLP.

The first step in tapping into the power of an NLP community is to either locate or establish one. If you are starting, online forums dedicated to NLP are a good starting point. Platforms like NLP Collective or The NLP Forum offer vibrant discussion boards where practitioners share experiences, advice, and resources; for those who prefer face-to-face interactions, local meetup groups can be found on websites like Meetup.com, where NLP enthusiasts regularly gather for workshops, practice sessions, and networking events. These meetings can be invaluable for building real-world connections and learning directly from experienced practitioners. Additionally, joining professional NLP networks like the Association for Neuro-Linguistic Programming (ANLP) provides access to a global community and skilled resources, including journals, conferences, and certification opportunities.

Active engagement is vital to maximizing its benefits once you are part of an NLP community. Participating in discussion groups, whether online or in person, allows you to engage more deeply with specific NLP topics and techniques. These discussions often challenge your understanding and push you to refine your approaches. Attending community events keeps you updated on the latest NLP developments and provides a platform to present your work, receiving constructive feedback from peers. Volunteering within these communities by organizing events or leading training sessions can further enhance your profile and give back to the community that supports your growth. Such activities deepen your knowledge and hone your leadership and communication skills, critical competencies in any NLP practitioner's toolkit.

The impact of a well-supported NLP community is best illustrated through success stories that highlight the practical benefits of such engagement. Take, for instance, the case of a regional NLP community in Seattle. Initially a small group, it grew significantly in size and scope within a few years, mainly due to an active leadership team that prioritized regular workshops and open communication channels between members. This community helped its members stay at the forefront of NLP techniques and collaborated on a multi-year project that integrated NLP into local schools, assisting educators in improving student engagement and learning outcomes.

Another example is an online NLP forum that started a monthly challenge where members apply specific NLP techniques to their personal or professional lives and share their results. This initiative kept the community engaged and created a rich repository of real-life case studies, showcasing the versatility and effectiveness of NLP across various contexts. Such collective knowledge significantly enhances individual and group expertise and provides a solid foundation for new members to build upon.

The value of building or joining an NLP support community lies in its impact on your personal and professional development. These communities provide a supportive network that motivates continuous learning and improvement, offers opportunities for collaboration, and amplifies the effects of NLP through shared experiences and successes. As you advance in your NLP journey, remember that your growth is amplified by the knowledge you acquire, the connections you make, and the support you give and receive within your NLP community.

8.4 Ethics and Responsibility in NLP Practice

In Neurolinguistic Programming (NLP), where the power to influence and transform lives can be significant, the commitment to ethical practice is not just a professional obligation but a moral imperative. The ethical foundations of NLP are built on the principles of respect, integrity, and responsibility. As practitioners, it is paramount to uphold these values, ensuring that our interventions and interactions promote the welfare and respect the autonomy of our clients and the community. We must recognize that our techniques can have significant and lasting effects on the individuals we work with, making ethical vigilance crucial in every aspect of our practice.

Navigating the ethical landscape in NLP involves understanding and managing several potential dilemmas arising from the practitioner-client relationship. One common ethical challenge is the risk of dependency, where clients may become overly reliant on their NLP practitioner instead of developing their coping mechanisms and resources. To handle this responsibly, it is vital to foster independence in clients, encouraging them to apply NLP techniques independently and gradually reducing the frequency of sessions as they gain confidence in their abilities. Another ethical dilemma involves confidentiality and boundary issues. NLP practitioners must ensure that all client information is confidential and that professional boundaries are maintained. This includes being transparent about the nature of the relationship from the outset and avoiding dual relationships that could impair objectivity and professional judgment.

Maintaining professional integrity and credibility in NLP practice requires adherence to established ethical guidelines and continuous self-monitoring. Transparency with clients is a cornerstone of ethical practice. This involves being honest about one's qualifications, the potential benefits, and the limitations of NLP. It is also crucial to provide clients with all the information they need to make informed decisions about their involvement in NLP processes. Additionally, NLP practitioners should commit to their ongoing professional development and stay abreast of new research, techniques, and ethical standards. This commitment not only enhances the quality of care provided to clients but also contributes to the credibility and reputation of NLP as a discipline.

The role of supervision and peer review in maintaining ethical standards cannot be overstated. Regular supervision sessions allow NLP practitioners to reflect on their practice, gain insights from more experienced colleagues, and ensure that they adhere to ethical norms. Peer review, meanwhile, offers a platform for practitioners to present their work to peers for critique and feedback. These processes encourage transparency and accountability, helping practitioners identify areas for improvement and prevent potential ethical violations. Moreover, they foster a culture of continuous learning and ethical vigilance within the NLP community, which is essential for the growth and sustainability of the practice.

To illustrate the importance of these ethical practices, consider the following scenarios where adherence to ethical guidelines played a crucial role:

1. **A case of boundary management:** An NLP practitioner working with a client on relationship issues found out they both frequented the same social club. Recognizing the potential for boundary issues, the practitioner discussed this with the client

and agreed to maintain a professional relationship, avoiding social interactions at the club to prevent conflicts of interest.

2. **A scenario involving informed consent:** During an NLP session, the practitioner planned to use a new technique that involved regression. Knowing the potential sensitivity of such a technique, they first explained its nature, benefits, and risks to the client, ensuring they had all the necessary information to give informed consent before proceeding.

3. **An instance of professional integrity:** A potential client approached a practitioner who wanted quick fixes for deep-seated behavioral issues. The practitioner explained that while NLP provides valuable tools for change, it requires commitment and time to be truly effective. They assessed what could be realistically achieved, upholding transparency and integrity.

These examples underscore the critical importance of ethical considerations in NLP practice. By adhering to moral principles and actively engaging in supervision and peer review, practitioners safeguard their clients' interests and well-being and enhance their professional growth and the integrity of the NLP field.

8.5 Future Trends in NLP: What's Next?

As the landscape of Neurolinguistic Programming continues to expand, it's crucial to stay ahead of emerging trends shaping this dynamic field's future. Advances in technology and shifts in societal needs drive significant innovations in NLP, paving the way for even more beneficial impacts across various sectors. Understanding these trends prepares you to adapt and innovate and enhances your ability to apply NLP techniques creatively and effectively.

One of the most exciting developments in NLP is integrating digital technology, particularly artificial intelligence (AI) and machine learning. These technologies are starting to play pivotal roles in automating and enhancing NLP techniques, making them more accessible and tailored to individual needs. For instance, AI-driven platforms are being developed to analyze speech patterns and body language more efficiently, providing NLP practitioners with deeper insights into their clients' emotional and psychological states. This technology enables practitioners to offer personalized coaching sessions based on precise, data-driven analyses. Additionally, machine learning algorithms are being used to refine NLP models, ensuring they are continuously improved based on new data and outcomes. This enhances the effectiveness of NLP interventions and accelerates individuals' personal growth using these refined models.

The impact of digital technology on NLP extends beyond individual practice. It also transforms how NLP training and therapy are delivered. For example, virtual reality (VR) creates immersive environments where practitioners can train and apply NLP techniques in a controlled yet realistic setting. This application is particularly beneficial in educational and therapeutic contexts where experiential learning is crucial. VR simulations can mimic various social interactions and emotional scenarios, allowing practitioners and clients to practice and master NLP techniques in safe, repeatable environments. Using VR and other digital tools in NLP enhances the learning experience and makes it more engaging and applicable to real-world situations.

The expansion of NLP into new domains and industries is another trend that is gaining momentum. As organizations recognize the value of psychological and emotional insights in achieving business success, NLP is increasingly incorporated into digital health, education technology, and organizational behavior. In digital health, NLP techniques improve patient communication and enhance therapeutic outcomes. By understanding patients' language patterns and emotional responses, healthcare providers can tailor their interactions to meet their needs better and improve treatment plan compliance. In education, NLP is applied to develop more effective teaching tools and techniques, enhancing student engagement and learning outcomes. Similarly, in organizational behavior, NLP is helping companies cultivate better leadership, improve team dynamics, and boost employee well-being and productivity.

Preparing for these future developments requires a proactive approach. Staying informed about NLP's latest research findings and technological advancements is essential. Regularly attending industry conferences, subscribing to relevant journals, and participating in online forums can keep you updated on new insights and innovations. Additionally, experimenting with emerging technologies and applying new NLP techniques in your practice will enhance your skills and provide you with firsthand experience of their potential impacts. Building partnerships with technologists and researchers can further enrich your understanding and application of advanced NLP tools, ensuring your practice remains cutting-edge.

As NLP continues to evolve, its applications will likely become more diverse, and its techniques will be more integrated with technology. By embracing these changes and preparing for future developments, you can ensure that your NLP practice remains relevant and continues to impact the lives of those you work with significantly. Whether it's through adopting new technologies, exploring new domains, or continually updating your skills, the future of NLP promises even greater possibilities for personal and professional growth. Embracing these opportunities will enhance your practice and contribute to the broader evolution of NLP as a vital tool for human development.

8.6 Leveraging Digital Platforms for NLP Learning and Growth

In an era where digital technology is at the forefront of educational and professional development, leveraging these tools for Neurolinguistic Programming (NLP) offers unprecedented advantages. The digital landscape provides many tools and platforms that transform how NLP practitioners learn, apply, and teach these essential techniques. From mobile apps that offer on-the-go learning opportunities to virtual reality simulations that provide immersive training environments, the digital resources available today make NLP more accessible and applicable than ever before.

The first step for practitioners eager to integrate these digital tools into their NLP practice is to explore the variety of available apps. Mobile applications such as NLP Coach and iNLP Center provide users access to numerous NLP resources, including interactive exercises, audio lessons, and tracking features that monitor personal growth and goal achievement. These apps are designed to support both novice and seasoned NLP practitioners, offering easy-to-navigate interfaces and customizable learning experiences. Furthermore, webinars and virtual workshops conducted by NLP experts allow practitioners to learn new techniques and strategies from the comfort of their homes or offices. These sessions often include live interactions, allowing for real-time feedback and discussion and significantly enriching the learning experience.

Meanwhile, virtual reality (VR) technology redefines the boundaries of NLP training and practice. VR simulations can create realistic scenarios where practitioners can apply NLP techniques in a controlled yet lifelike environment. This is particularly beneficial for skills such as public speaking, negotiation, or therapy, where the immersive nature of VR helps simulate real-life interactions and challenges. Practitioners can experiment with different techniques and receive immediate feedback within the simulation, facilitating rapid improvement and confidence in applying these skills in actual situations. Integrating these digital tools effectively into daily practice involves familiarizing oneself with their functionalities and consistently incorporating these technologies into training regimes and client sessions. This might mean using VR as a regular training tool or integrating app-based exercises into homework for clients.

The benefits of engaging with online learning networks and virtual communities are extensive. These platforms facilitate a continuous exchange of knowledge and support among NLP practitioners worldwide. Members can share experiences, discuss challenges, and exchange insights, leading to enhanced understanding and application of NLP. Furthermore, these communities often provide access to various resources, including case studies, research papers, and expert advice. For practitioners, participation in these networks not only broadens their knowledge base but also provides emotional and professional support, helping them to stay motivated and informed about the latest developments in the field of NLP.

To demonstrate the practical impact of these digital platforms, consider the following case studies of successful digital integration in NLP training and practice:

1. **The Virtual Practice Room:** A group of NLP practitioners developed a VR simulation called the Virtual Practice Room, designed for practicing interpersonal skills. Within this virtual environment, users could interact with avatars controlled by AI to simulate different social interactions. The system instantly generated Feedback on their performance, providing users

with specific insights into their communication style and effectiveness. This tool allowed practitioners to refine their skills in a risk-free environment, making noticeable improvements in real-world interactions.

2. **The NLP Learning App:** An NLP training center developed a mobile app to complement their courses. The app included interactive content, quizzes, and a community forum where students could discuss lessons and share insights. The app allowed for an ongoing engagement with NLP concepts, reinforcing learning and providing a platform for continuous professional development. Users reported higher levels of satisfaction and better retention of information compared to traditional learning methods alone.

These case studies highlight how embracing digital tools and platforms can significantly enhance NLP learning and practice. Integrating these technologies into your routine can improve your skills and provide others with more effective, engaging, and personalized NLP training.

As we close this exploration of digital advancements in NLP, we recognize that the journey of learning and applying NLP is ever-evolving. The tools and techniques may change, but the core objective remains steadfast: to harness the power of NLP to transform lives. As you continue navigating the vast resources and possibilities, remember that each digital tool, each online course, and each virtual interaction is a stepping stone towards greater mastery and a deeper understanding of the human mind. Let these digital advancements be your allies in pursuing excellence in NLP.

AFTERWORD

It is essential to reflect on the potential of neurolinguistic programming (NLP). Throughout this book, we've emphasized how NLP offers robust personal and professional transformation tools. By reprogramming our thought patterns, enhancing our communication abilities, and fostering an environment of success and happiness, NLP stands as a growth and development pillar. The potential for growth with NLP is limitless, inspiring hope and excitement.

We have navigated through the most impactful NLP concepts and techniques, such as the power of reframing perspectives, the critical role of representational systems, the effectiveness of anchoring and visualization, and the utility of the Meta-Model and Milton Model. Each tool provides a unique lens through which we can view and alter our world, enhancing personal efficacy and interpersonal relationships.

NLP strategies are not just theoretical knowledge but a practical and valuable skill set that can significantly improve our daily interactions and help us manage life's challenges more effectively. This practicality ensures that NLP is not just a concept to be understood but a tool to be actively applied within various domains of life, empowering you to take control of your personal and professional growth.

An essential aspect of using NLP is the adherence to ethical practices. As we wield these powerful tools, we must do so responsibly, ensuring our actions always align with the highest ethical standards. This commitment to integrity safeguards our practices and enriches the lives of those we interact with, fostering a community of trust and respect.

For those who seek to master NLP, the journey does not end with the last page of this book. I encourage you to commit to lifelong learning and to actively practice the NLP techniques that bring you the most success. Remember, this is not just about learning but about doing. I wrote this book out of a personal interest in NLP—I am not an NLP therapist— believing that the techniques hold value and that you, dear reader, may benefit from actively applying them.

Now, I urge you to take these tools and techniques into your own hands. Apply what you've learned and experiment with these strategies in your daily life and professional encounters. The benefits you stand to gain—enhanced personal insights, improved relationships, and a more successful career—can be tremendous. You have the power to transform your life with NLP.

Reflecting on my journey with NLP, I am reminded of how it has enriched my life and career. From sharpening my decision-making skills to improving my interactions with others, NLP-type affirmations, reframing, and anchoring have aided my personal and professional development. For instance, when faced with a challenging decision, I used the 'six-step reframing' technique to reframe my perspective and make a more informed choice. NLP represents a set of mental technologies that many people have found effective. With discipline, these methods can indeed reprogram our minds.

However, it's important to note that my literature review

does not reveal a scientific consensus that NLP produces clinical results reliably. As a 2012 UK National Health Service study put it, the reason may be that the NLP practitioners have not been systematically producing research results (Sturt et al., 2012). The study found the NLP clinical results statistically inconclusive. This suggests that while NLP can be a powerful tool, it may not be a one-size-fits-all solution, and its effectiveness can vary from person to person.

Finally, I have used NLP techniques within the context of my Christian faith. It helps to believe in a God who will help you when confronted with seemingly intractable problems; being able to "give it to God" to resolve—while working by our own methods—has been the ultimate comfort (Middleton, 2024). This is not to say that NLP is a religious practice, but rather that it can be used in conjunction with one's faith to enhance personal development. The Universe is conscious and will help you if you ask nicely.

Thank you for joining me on this fascinating journey through the philosophy and practice of neurolinguistic programming. I am grateful for your time and engagement. As you apply these principles and techniques, I encourage you to have faith and confidence in yourself and your ability to reprogram your mind.

A REQUEST

Dear Reader,

If you have found value in this book, please share your experience by writing a review on Amazon. The algorithm rules at Amazon, and your review will enable more people to find this book.

If you are reading an ebook, please click this link to be taken to your review page.

If you are reading a print book, point your phone's camera at the QR code below to be taken to your review page. Thank you!

ANNOTATED BIBLIOGRAPHY

Bandler, R., & Grinder, J. (1975). The Structure of Magic I: A Book About Language and Therapy. Science and Behavior Books. Summary: This foundational work introduces the concepts of neurolinguistic programming (NLP) and its applications in therapy. It explains how language and thought patterns influence human behavior and provides techniques for therapeutic interventions.

Bandler, R., & Grinder, J. (1976). The Structure of Magic II: A Book About Communication and Change. Science and Behavior Books. Summary: Continuing from the first volume, this book focuses on the communication strategies and techniques used in NLP to facilitate personal change and improve interpersonal interactions.

Bandler, R., & Grinder, J. (1979). Frogs into Princes: Neuro Linguistic Programming. Real People Press. Summary: This book offers a more practical guide to NLP, presenting techniques for improving communication, changing unhelpful behaviors, and achieving personal goals.

Begum, H., Anjomshoaa, A., Espinales, K., Moreno, M., El-Ashry, E., Nazim, S., & Yousaf, A. (2021). The effect of neurolinguistic programming on academic achievement, emotional intelligence, and critical thinking of EFL learners. Frontiers in Psychology. Retrieved from https://www.frontiersin.org/articles/10.3389/fpsyg.2021.623214/full Summary: This study investigates the impact of NLP on English as a Foreign Language (EFL) learners' academic performance, emotional intelligence, and critical thinking skills, demonstrating positive outcomes in these areas.

Bhugra, D., & Tasman, A. (2024). Neurolinguistic programming: Old wine in new glass. Indian Journal of Psychiatry. Retrieved from https://journals.lww.com/indianjpsychiatry/fulltext/2024/66030/neurolinguistic_programming__old_wine_in_new_glass.10.aspx Summary: This article provides a critical review of NLP, examining its historical development and current applications, and questioning its effectiveness and scientific validity.

Brandeis, D. (2024). Pseudoscience: A Review of Neuro-Linguistic Programming (NLP). Behavioral Today. Retrieved from https://www.behavioraltoday.com/articles/pseudoscience-a-review-of-neuro-linguistic-programming-nlp Summary: This review critically examines the claims and scientific evidence behind NLP, categorizing it as a pseudoscience due to the lack of empirical support for many of its techniques.

Carey, J., & Churches, R. (2013). Neuro-Linguistic Programming for Dummies. John Wiley & Sons. **Summary:** This accessible guide introduces the basic concepts and techniques of NLP, providing practical advice for applying NLP in various personal and professional contexts.

Dilts, R., Grinder, J., Bandler, R., & DeLozier, J. (1980). Neuro-Linguistic Programming: Volume I. Meta Publications. **Summary:** This volume provides a comprehensive overview of NLP's foundational theories and methodologies, detailing its applications in therapy and personal development.

Dilts, R. (1999). Sleight of Mouth: The Magic of Conversational Belief Change. Meta Publications. **Summary:** This book focuses on advanced NLP techniques for influencing and changing beliefs through conversation, offering a range of strategies for effective communication.

Gray, R. M. (2011). Transforming Futures: The Brooklyn Program Facilitator Manual. Crown House Publishing. **Summary:** This manual provides a detailed guide for facilitators of the Brooklyn Program, an NLP-based intervention aimed at helping individuals transform their futures through structured exercises and techniques.

Gray, R. M. (2013). About Addictions: Notes from Psychology, Neuroscience, and NLP. Crown House Publishing. **Summary:** This book explores the intersection of psychology, neuroscience, and NLP in understanding and treating addictions, offering insights and practical approaches for practitioners.

Grinder, J., & Bandler, R. (1981). Trance-Formations: Neuro-Linguistic Programming and the Structure of Hypnosis. Real People Press. **Summary:** This work integrates NLP with hypnosis, presenting techniques for using hypnotic states to facilitate personal change and therapeutic outcomes.

Keezhatta, M. S., & Omar, N. A. (2019). Neuro-linguistic programming: A systematic review of the effects on health outcomes. British Journal of General Practice. Retrieved from https://bjgp.org/content/early/recent **Summary:** This systematic review assesses the impact of NLP on various health outcomes, summarizing the evidence for its effectiveness and highlighting areas for further research.

Middleton, E. (2024). Harmony Within: How to Achieve Holistic Wellness. Kindle Direct Publishing. **Summary:** This book offers a comprehensive approach to achieving holistic wellness through integrating physical, mental, and spiritual health practices.

Muniandy, M., Rasyid, N. M., & Abdul Razak, N. (2023). Development of neuro linguistic programming module for golf athletes: A needs analysis. Journal of Learning Theory and Methodology. **Summary:** This study outlines the development of an NLP module tailored for golf athletes, aimed at improving their performance through mental conditioning and strategic thinking.

O'Connor, J., & Seymour, J. (1990). Introducing Neuro-Linguistic Programming: Psychological Skills for Understanding and Influencing People. HarperCollins. Summary: This introductory text presents the fundamental principles of NLP, offering practical techniques for understanding and influencing human behavior.

O'Connor, J., & Seymour, J. (1990). Introducing Neuro-Linguistic Programming: Psychological Skills for Understanding and Influencing People. Thorsons. Summary: This edition provides a comprehensive overview of NLP, with practical exercises and applications for personal and professional development.

Passmore, J., & Rowson, T. (2019). Neuro-linguistic programming: A critical review of NLP research and the application of NLP in coaching. International Coaching Psychology Review, 14(1), 57-69. Summary: This review critically examines the research on NLP and its application in coaching, discussing the evidence for its effectiveness and limitations.

PLOS ONE. (2021). The eyes don't have it: Lie detection and neuro-linguistic programming. PLOS ONE. Retrieved from https://doi.org/10.1371/journal.pone.0040259 Summary: This study investigates the use of NLP techniques in lie detection, specifically examining the validity of eye movement patterns as indicators of deception.

Purnama, Y., Sobirov, B., Ino, L., Handayani, F., & Al-Awawdeh, N. (2023). Neuro-linguistic programming as an instructional strategy to enhance foreign language teaching. Studies in Media and Communication, 11(5), 50-59. Summary: This article explores the application of NLP strategies in foreign language teaching, highlighting how NLP techniques can enhance language acquisition and instructional effectiveness.

Rogers, C. (2023). The concept of neuro-linguistic programming in improving the receptive skills in English. Rupkatha Journal on Interdisciplinary Studies in Humanities, 13(1), 112-139. Summary: This paper examines the role of NLP in enhancing English language learners' receptive skills, discussing various techniques and their impact on listening and reading comprehension.

Singh, R. K., & Kaur, J. (2023). Neuro Linguistic Programming: An Effective Tool for Teaching. International Journal of Scientific Research and Engineering Trends. Retrieved from https://ijsrst.com/IJSRST2310172 Summary: This study investigates the application of NLP in teaching, demonstrating its effectiveness in improving educational outcomes and student engagement.

Sturt, J., Ali, S., Robertson, W., Metcalfe, D., Grove, A., Bourne, C., & Bridle, C. (2012). Neurolinguistic programming: A systematic review of the effects on health outcomes. *British Journal of General Practice, 62*(604), e757-e764. https://doi.org/10.3399/bjgp12X658287 Summary: This systematic review by Sturt et al. examines the impact of Neurolinguistic Programming (NLP) on various health outcomes. The study analyzed data from multiple research articles to assess the effectiveness of NLP in improving physical and mental health. The review found limited high-quality evidence supporting the effectiveness of NLP, with most studies demonstrating methodological weaknesses. While some positive effects were reported, the overall evidence was inconclusive. The authors concluded that more rigorous research is needed to determine the potential health benefits of NLP.

Tosey, P., & Mathison, J. (2009). **Neuro-linguistic Programming: A Critical Appreciation for Managers and Developers. Palgrave Macmillan. Summary:** This book offers a critical analysis of NLP, focusing on its applications in management and personal development, and discussing its strengths and limitations.

Velichko, E., Ivanov, V., & Smirnov, A. (2023). **Scientific status of neuro-linguistic programming and discoursologic analysis of linguistic aspect. ResearchGate. Retrieved from https://www.researchgate.net/publica tion/366367467_Scientific_status_of_neuro-linguistic_program ming_and_discoursologic_analysis_of_linguistic_aspect Summary:** The article highlights the ongoing scientific debate regarding the legitimacy and effectiveness of NLP, delving into various linguistic aspects and critiquing current methodologies.

Wake, L., & Jackson, P. (2004). **Neurolinguistic Psychotherapy: A Postmodern Perspective. Routledge. Summary:** This book presents NLP within the context of psychotherapy, offering a postmodern perspective on its techniques and their application in therapeutic settings.

Witkowski, T. (2010). **Thirty-five years of research on Neuro-Linguistic Programming. NLP research data base. State of the art or pseudoscientific decoration? Polish Psychological Bulletin, 41**(2), 58-66. https://doi. org/10.2478/v10059-010-0008-0 Summary: This review summarizes 35 years of research on NLP, evaluating its scientific credibility and questioning whether it is a legitimate field of study or a pseudoscientific practice.

Zaharia, C., Reiner, M., & Schutz, P. (2015). <u>Evidence-based neuro linguistic psychotherapy: A meta analysisiPsychiatria Danubina, 27</u>(4),<u>_355-3632</u> <u>Summary:</u> This meta-analysis by Zaharia, Reiner, and Schutz examines the effectiveness of neuro-linguistic psychotherapy (NLPt) using evidence-based research. The study aggregates data from multiple studies to evaluate the therapeutic outcomes of NLPt. The findings suggest that NLPt is an effective intervention for various psychological conditions, demonstrating significant improvements in mental health outcomes compared to control groups. The authors conclude that NLPt has a solid evidence base, supporting its use as a viable therapeutic approach. However, they also call for further research to strengthen the evidence and address any methodological limitations in the existing studies.

Zhang, X., Davarpanah, N., & Izadpanah, S. (2023). **The effect of neurolinguistic programming on academic achievement, emotional intelligence, and critical thinking of EFL learners. Frontiers in Psychology. Summary:** This study investigates the impact of NLP on EFL learners' academic performance, emotional intelligence, and critical thinking skills, demonstrating positive outcomes in these areas.

Zhang, L., & Wang, Y. (2022). **Language Learning With Neurolinguistic Programming. Journal of Language Teaching and Research. Retrieved from** https://jltr.academypublication.com/index.php/jltr/article/view/4982 **Summary:** This paper explores the application of NLP in language learning, discussing how NLP techniques can facilitate better language acquisition and improve communication skills.

ABOUT THE AUTHOR

Elliott Middleton, PhD, is a former university professor and decision scientist for some of the world's largest financial institutions. He lives with his family in the Nashville, Tennessee, area.